Finding Value In Horse Racing
First Edition

Written by

© Isaac Robathan

Dedication

Peter Robson, Western Australia

Peter and I spent many happy days at the races in Perth, and even more hours looking at ways to beat the bookies. Thanks for the memories Pete, and the inspiration to keep going no matter what life throws at us.

Contents

About the Author

My interest in horses started when I was just 3 years old. I was the youngest in my family and my mother brought us up on her own. We never had much in those days and many of my early memories have faded with the passage of time. But one remains at the forefront of my mind: Christmas of 1956. It was a time for celebration and enjoying what life could afford to offer. One beloved toy that I specifically remember from that year is a small blue felt pad which had things like felt Triangles, Circles and Squares etc on, the other two things were one Black felt horse and one White felt horses. My mother would often tell me how fascinated I had been with these two horses, and how I used to throw them on the pad as if they were racing each other. I remember the two horses very clearly. As a seven-year-old my mother took me to Uttoxeter races, and that was it, the racing bug bit me.

I was fascinated with those huge horses in the paddock and loved watching them race around the track. Every time there was a weekend meeting, I would be there, parking my push bike up at Redfern's farm. I would then nip across the track under the rails and into the stand area before anyone else even turned up.

I was eleven years old when I sat on my first Racehorse at Reg Hollinshead stable in upper Longdon, Rugeley. I cycled over twenty miles every weekend on Saturday and Sunday just to be close to Racehorses and watch them exercise.

I did a paper round so I could buy the Sporting Life every weekend. I would read and study the Saturday paper every day of the week until the next weekend's paper was out. There was no Sunday racing in those days.

I left school as soon as I could and started my career in racing, Riding, Racing and Schooling horses. Racing was my life.

About the Author

One Cold winters day in February my perfect life took a sudden turn. Schooling a young horse over fences he slipped on take-off. He caught the top of the fence, somersaulted, and buried me in the turf. That day was a massive turning point in my life. It was 18 months before I eventually got back in the saddle. racing seemed liked a distant memory. My love for horses never changed but the path I was taking did.

I Emigrated to Australia in 1983, where I met Peter Robson. Peter was fascinated with Racing and Data; we struck up a great friendship. Going to the races in Perth every Saturday. In the evenings we would discuss the days racing and talk about selection methods. I wrote a Database for all horses and courses in Western Australia. When at the races I would stand at the pre parade ring and select what I considered to be the fittest horse in the paddock. We did extremely well in those days.

Circumstances brought me back to the UK where I continued to go to the Races as often as possible, taking up my favourite spot by the pre parade ring. In those days I produced my own ratings and kept my own database. Since returning to the UK, I have had several thoroughbreds of my own now shared with my wife who I am lucky enough shares my passion for horses. Also, on the plus side she is excellent at spotting and diagnosing the slightest fault in a horse's gait. The number of times she has diagnosed our own horses and brought them back from the brink is incredible.

Introduction

These days there is plenty of information to help punters. Software like those named below.

RaceformInteractive.com: A huge amount information that can be manipulated in many ways to suit a users preferences. Maybe to much information for the casual user but brilliant for the semi pro or professional gambler.

Timeform.com: started by the late Phil Bull a well-known professional punter back in his day. Timeform produce excellent time figures and are well known throughout the racing Industry. Quite highly priced but they have an excellent reputation within the industry.

Proform.com: maybe more complicated to use. It may take time to understand it, however people get decent results using this software.

Horseracebase.com: produced by Chris Bagnall and his team. Horseracebase is brilliant for the casual backer and professional alike, literally thousands of ways to manipulate data, user friendly too.

They all do much the same some are more complicated than others some more expensive than others. I use Horseracebase for my form study, the information in this book is taken mainly from data supplied by Horseracebase. Chris has kindly given me permission to reprint pages from Horseracebase to show how I use different ways of finding potential value for money selections.

Horseracebase

Horseracebase

Whatever software you use you should be able to adapt it to do things similar to the way I use Horseracebase.

The Ratings produced by Horseracebase are excellent on their own. They are made up of 20 Columns of information. They show the horses' last ten races. There is a Leveller column for horses that have had one or two races. There are columns for Trainers, Jockeys, Stallions etc. All these figures go to make up the total rating for each horse. I will only use, at the most the last three or four races.

Horseracebase gives us a mountain of information on Trainers, Jockeys etc as well as every horses racing career. I use some of this information, but it would be impossible to use it all.

Seasoned users of Horseracebase will probably use the information in different ways too. and that is fine there is more than one way of interpreting form.

I will only be showing data that is relevant to the race that we are covering at the time.

Systems

Systems

I want to point out right now there is NO GET RICH QUICK SCHEME In horse racing. Profits come from Study, Experience and Homework. You need to enjoy what you do there is no need to make it encompass all that you do. If you enjoy your form study, you will be more successful. I do not need to tell you what a system is. There are plenty of people selling their ideas of good systems. Punters that use software will create their own systems. A few may be profitable many will not be. Personally, I do not use systems in the conventional way. That is, I do not use systems to find winners or systems to find horses to Lay. I use systems to find losers now that may sound foolish. We can all find losers without creating a system for it.

When I create a system, I look for patterns. In the main I am looking for patterns of losing favourites. If I can find a system that tells me the races and the condition of races where favourites get beaten often. I then know there is something in the race that I could get exceptional value for. Of course, it is not possible to find something in every race that pops up in a particular system. First, I need to decide if the favourite really is vulnerable, if so, I go about looking for something else that has an excellent chance in the race. Then I know I will have value in the race. If you are getting value your chance of making a profit overall is enhanced.

I have no problem with people that look for systems to find winners. One of my racing friends has a particularly good system where he backs odds on favourites. He does very well out of it too. Obviously, he risks a great deal of money for a smaller reward, but he does make it pay. I am the opposite side of the coin I prefer to risk little for a greater reward.

Systems

The one problem I have with systems is that many are based on historical data. Over a minimum of 10 years or so. To evaluate a system over a 10 year or even a 20-year period you need to leave a year or two out. When you think you have the results you were looking for and your system has shown a profit every year add those years back in. If those years show a profit too you are onto something. If those years, then show a loss. You are just making your system fit the data. It is worth you testing your system in this way before parting with any money.

Horseracebase gives you an exceptional way of testing systems. In the systems Performance Report, you can run your system from the saved date of your system. It is worth letting them run for a few months and then see if your system is producing the results that you expect.

Around 2015 I developed a system that looked for Fillies that start favourite on All Weather tracks and are vulnerable. The reason I did this is because I know that Fillies do not perform as well as Colts or Geldings on certain types of surfaces. I modified it in 2021 to this day it keeps showing me favourites that have a high percentage chance of getting beaten. Since I modified it there have been fifty-six selections only 9 of those fillies have won, around 16.07%. When favourites win around 28%-32% of the time this seems to be a brilliant system, and it gives me an edge in those races.

As I said previously, I use that system to look for something else in the race that could beat the favourite filly. I do not need many systems like that to do very well when selecting horses from home.

Systems

Let us work through a practical example that has happened today whilst I have been drafting this book. We all know that the O'Brien's turn out plenty of winners particularly when it comes to group races. Today Joseph Patrick O'Brien has a runner at Naas. Joseph is one trainer that I admire greatly. Vastly under rated as a jockey now turns out top class horses in top class races as a trainer. The trouble is everyone knows it; therefore, his runners are not value for their price..

Joseph's runners at the time of writing that start between 1.4 and 2.00 which is 4/5 and Evens stands at 46.79% winners for the last six years. Therefore 53.21% of his runners that start as favourite between those two prices get beaten. Therefore, there is scope to find something else in the race that will be at a value for money price.

It is worth checking these races to see if there is anything in the race with form close enough to his noticeably short priced favourite, that may come and either beat his runner or at least give it a run for its money. Sometimes you will not be able to find anything, and his horse will win. Or you do think you have something, and his horse still beats yours. However, you will have the Value for Money horse and if you are patient enough you will come out on top. Let us look at today's example in the 1:40 at Naas Joseph has an odds-on favourite that went off at 4/9. Let us see what else is in the race.

The ratings for the race are printed below. I have only reprinted from HRB the top 4 in the ratings table just to make this point.

Horse	Total	Odds	LR	2LR
Il Pellegrino (IRE)	175.1	4/9	80.4	0.0
Goal Exceeded	172.4	7/2	79.7	36.0
Take Me to The Church (IRE)	143.1	17/2	66.3	29.8
Bobbys Glory (IRE)	111.4	100/1	51.5	23.2

Systems

We can see from the ratings table that Il Pellegrino and Goal Exceeded are close in both their respective Total Ratings and more importantly in their last race ratings. Below I have printed my Ratings which brings all their last two ratings to 100%.

Horse	Total	Odds	LR	2LR
Il Pellegrino (IRE)	334.9	4/9	83.3	0.0
Take Me to The Church (IRE)	302.9	17/2	78.1	76.3
Goal Exceeded	274.4	7/2	86.8	53.1
Surpass and Shine (IRE)	196.1	!50/1	50.6	0.0

Now we can see that in the last race for each horse Goal Exceeded has a better rating than Il Pelegrino and he has an improved rating since his previous race.

The next thing to do is check the speed figures for the two produced by HRB. The table below shows their respective speed figures.

Horse	Total	Odds	L	2L
Il Pellegrino (IRE)	64.21	4/9	64.21	0
Take Me to The Church (IRE)	64.07	17/2	62.66	65.19
Goal Exceeded	63.03	7/2	64.83	60.79
Surpass and Shine (IRE)	52.66	150/1	52.66	0

On Speed figures Goal Exceeded's last race was better than Il Pelegrino's, not by much admittedly but still better. We can make the argument that Il Pelegrino has only had one race and is likely to improve.

Systems

 I know that Joseph turns his runners fit first time so there may not be a great deal of improvement. Whereas Goal Exceeded has now ran twice showing considerable improvement between the two runs. The Result

1st: Goal Exceeded 7/2

2nd: Take Me To The Church 17/2

3rd: Il Pelegrino 4/9

Another loser for J P O'Brien at 0dds on. There will be races where nothing comes close to the odds-on favourite. Meaning there will not always be a selection. This is what I mean by looking for systems to find losers something that may just get beaten. You can pick on any price for favourites run through all the trainers and you will see many top trainers horses with less than 50% win rate at odds on.

A.M Balding is another trainer whose horses regularly start at odds on, sometimes deserved often not, between July and August in 2023 he had seven odds on favourites in row that failed to win.

In the last ten-years there has not been one year where following horses starting between 1.4 and 2.0 have shown a profit at SP. Therefore, there is considerable opportunity to look for value elsewhere.

Ironically, Ireland has both the best and worst tracks for horses starting at odds-on, Punchestown, Ballinrobe and Roscommon around 70%+ of horses starting between 1.4 and 2.0 go on to win. Wexford, Clonmel and Fairyhouse only win around 30% of the time. Those three courses once went twelve consecutive losing odds-on favourites. A study as to why that is could prove to be profitable.

One reason that is clear and obvious, where there are more than fourteen or more runners in the race less than 50% win, but where there are less than fourteen runners then more than 50% win.

Systems

It is easy to create systems to find losing favourites on average favourites win 28% of the time in handicaps then clearly, they lose 72% of the time. In Non handicaps they win around 40% of the time so they lose 60% of the time. The knack is finding a system where the favourite loses more than those two averages. For example, Handicaps favourites on the All Weather at Newcastle, if they last ran at either Southwell or Dundalk, they only Win a fraction over 15% of the time once going on a losing streak of twenty-two without a single winner.

I keep two systems that look at trainers who bring their charges out in 3-5 days of a previous race and start favourite. The average win percentage is 33%. My first list is for those trainers whose horses go on to win a minimum of 40% of the time and have an even greater place percentage. I do not automatically back these. I do my homework and check to see their recent form in comparison to the rest of the field stacks up. If so, it may become a selection depending on the price plus other factors.

The other list is for trainers who bring their runners out within 3-5 days and start favourite but only manage to pull it off less than 20% of the time. I then do my homework on these races to see if I can find something that is likely to beat the favourite.

There was such a case on the 21st of August 2023 when D Carol ran Asmund at Catterick. Asmund started the 5/1(J/Fav) which was a particularly good price for him. It did not take a great deal of looking to find a better proposition and it was not the other (J/Fav). Looking at the ratings etc and doing a form check Mutanaaseq was well clear of Asmund. The icing on the cake was that he was only beaten by 1.4 lengths last time when finishing 4th. I mention later in the book about the value of horses that finish 4th, 5th, or 6th but close to the winner in a fast run race. Mutanaaseq went on to win at 8/1 with Asmund finishing second at 5/1.

Systems

That system once went twenty-three losing favourites in a row. Which gives me many opportunities to find something else in the race to challenge the favourite. Do not get me wrong I cannot always find something else to have an interest in. There are always plenty of other things to look at in a day. All I need to do is enjoy what I am doing and have a sack full of patience.

Another winning/losing system I use regularly is trainers that follow up a win with a winning favourite next time out. Plus of course a list of trainers that do not follow up a win with a winning favourite next time out. Horses that win their previous race then start favourite for their next race win approximately 32% of the time. Percentages are different for Handicap and Non-Handicap races of course, however overall, 32% is about average. My two lists contain trainers that achieve two in a row over 40% of the time. The one I take greatest interest in is trainers that do not achieve two in row and only achieve it less than 20% of the time. Of course, they still get their winners. It all depends on the form of the horses in the race, but it gives me an edge to look for something other than the favourite.

Of course, you need to thoroughly do your homework the winning trainers once went a run of fifteen races without another winning favourite. They also once went a run of ten winning favourites on the trot.

With HRB you can create thousands of these diverse ways to try to get the percentages in your favour.

Though you can create 100's of systems with HRB you are far better off working with a few to start with. You can make as many as you like but keep them inactive. You can still check the results from them in the systems performance report.

Systems

When creating systems always make sure you check the Profit/Loss at SP not the Betfair prices. You can create a system that makes huge profits on Betfair, but the Starting Price is still a negative. The reason for that is somewhere in your system either one or two horses have won at 20/1 or more and paid silly prices at Betfair SP. Those silly prices will throw the validity of your system out. You will find you have huge losing runs in such a system.

You can set up systems in HRB that automatically tell you if races you are interested in are on the days agenda. Too many systems set up like this would give you far too many races and horses to look at and could easily throw up several selections in one race. For example, if I am looking for a filly on the All Weather that is going to start as the favourite. I will resurrect that system. I do not have Seventy or Eighty systems giving me selections.

Of course, I do have many systems that I can work with I have my favourites then if there is time, I look at others usually I do not need to, the important thing is to update or delete any that are not doing what you originally thought they should.

Systems are usually based on hard facts based on historical data, they are an aid to help you find value for money selections, like the majority of my systems they do not have to pinpoint a particular runner, they can be an aid to look for value in the race also based on historical data.

For Example, the system I use for Fillies that start favourite in non-handicap races, when up against Colts and Geldings they often get beaten, particularly if they come from a stable either not in form or has a low percentage of winning favourites, checking the ratings and speed figures plus the other trainer's, you could easily come up with a selection that will give far better value.

Ratings

Ratings

The importance of ratings is a hotly debated subject. You either use them and rely on them or you ignore them. That will probably depend on how much you happen to win or lose by following your set of ratings.

To produce ratings across the whole spectrum of racing that continually make a profit at Starting Price year in year out is extremely difficult.

It is entirely possible to create a selective system that does make a profit from the top-rated horse.

Just as a quick example the table below shows the last 1000 races of a system I have just created in a few seconds.

I have taken 2023 flat season in the UK
Flat Handicaps
5-8 Runner favourites
Top Rated by HRB

Rank	Bets	Wins	Win%	Places	Places%	P/L
1	482	196	40.66%	297	61.62%	39.22
2	264	84	31.82%	143	54.17%	-10.33
3	162	45	27.78%	88	54.32%	-23.72
4	105	32	30.48%	57	54.29%	2.33
5	43	10	23.26%	21	48.84%	-8.59
6	29	8	27.59%	16	55.17%	0.09
7	4	0	0.00%	2	50.00%	-4.00
8	3	1	33.33%	2	66.67%	0.75

This shows a profit of £39.22 to a £1 stake with a win Percentage of 40.66%. I could easily better this in many ways, but this took less than 30 seconds to set up.

The data on its own without the Ratings would have made a SP loss of -£120.17. The data was taken in August 2023.

Ratings

Just that demonstration alone should tell you that selective systems do have a place for ratings. The System of Favourites in 5-8 runners' races on the UK Flat would have produced a loss. If someone just created that system, they would have dumped it as not profitable. When you marry it up with ratings as good as those produced by HRB just the top-rated horse makes it profitable.

For me HRB Standard ratings are good enough. Top rated in Flat Handicaps in the UK win 23% of the time. Non-Handicap races 30% of the time. That is all runners wherever they are in the market. The way ratings are set up in HRB is perfect for comparing runners with each other and looking back at previous races to see if horses are improving or falling away. The only change I make to HRB standard is to create my own that I call my HRB Check. That is, I take HRB standard and instead of decreasing by a percentage for the second last race, third last race etc. I make every race 100% then I can easily see if a horse is progressing or not. I first look at HRB Standard then at my checker that gives me a particularly good feel for the race.

You need to use ratings in conjunction with other data that you may have access too. HRB has in recent years due to popular demand by their clients produced speed ratings.

Once again, they leave nothing to chance the speed ratings they produce are as good as any. HRB create their own standard times that you can manipulate anyway you want. For me they are good enough as they are. Later I will run through how I use both ratings and speed ratings for my selections.

Ratings and Speed Ratings do not always go hand in hand, a good rating does not mean there will be a good speed rating and vice versa, you may need to check if either the speed rating or the rating is warranted. Sometimes this is an easy exercise to do other times it will take a bit more research, but the work you put in will be well worth it.

Ratings

After looking at both sets of ratings, I would not select just from that data alone. I read my comments on Trainers for each horse. I look to see if there is a pattern that I have noticed in certain trainers that is likely to have a bearing on the outcome of the race. If there is, I evaluate the horse, if I discount it then fine. If there are two or more, which happens often then I would discount the race and move on.

This is most likely to happen in Nurseries where several runners have had three maiden or novice runs. Quite often they sprout new legs when going handicapping, two or more such runners can catch you out.

You can use ratings any way you want. I will run through my way, which I find highly successful, you may develop your own way of using them.

This book is for win betting for the UK and Ireland, covering the Flat, All-Weather and National Hunt racing. I have touched on place betting later in the book.

Flat racing and All-Weather racing are similar, you need a different mindset for National Hunt Racing. There are of course professionals that concentrate solely on National Hunt Racing, some concentrate on handicap chases only, their reasoning behind that is they get to know a great deal about the horses as the majority would have had a flat career plus a hurdling career, before going chasing, there is much to appreciate about that approach.

I will initially run through how I make selections using ratings on the flat and All-Weather racing.

A race that I looked at recently for a selection is a Handicap at Salisbury over 1Mile on the 7th of September 2023. I do not usually invest in races that are tight between two runners. I will run through my thinking on the runners in the race and how I concluded to select a contestant.

Ratings

Thu 7th Sep 2023
4.45 Salisbury (5 runners)
Madar Corporation Handicap
1m (1760 yards)
Class 3, Good To Firm, 3yo+, Win: £9450
Avg OR : 84, Median OR : 85
Straight, Stall Positioning : Far Side

This is the information on the race provided by HRB

HRB Standard Ratings

Horse	Total	Odds	LR	2LR
Just Bring it	196.2	2/1	111.0	23.6
Resolute Man	173.8	7/2	78.5	33.8
Garden Route	171.4	5/4	77.3	33.9
Sly Madam	164.3	12/1	70.2	34.6
Oj Lifestyle	121.9	28/1	52.4	24.3

Just Bring It is 20+ points ahead here on Standard Ratings, earlier in the day Power of Darkness won an Apprentice Handicap, Power of Darkness ran in the same race that Just Bring It won previously and finished twelfth.

HRB to 100%

Horse	Total	Odds	LR	2LR
Just Bring it	373.8	2/1	107.3	74.3
Resolute Man	358.8	7/2	85	84.3
Garden Route	352.1	5/4	80.5	89.6
Sly Madam	341.3	12/1	83.0	82.3
Oj Lifestyle	232.4	28/1	56.2	44.0

Ratings

You can see that Just Bring It is far above the rest on his last run. We will need to find out why. Let us look at the Speed Ratings.

Speed ratings

Horse	Total	Odds	LR	2LR
Just Bring it	75.8	2/1	76.72	71.17
Resolute Man	74.49	7/2	77.95	78.15
Garden Route	67.37	5/4	72.28	68.12
Sly Madam	65.09	12/1	68.33	69.85
Oj Lifestyle	62.08	28/1	57.07	49.27

Just Bring Its ratings are high because in his last race he won a £23K Class 3 race. Garden Route the 5/4 favourite ran in a £52K Class 2 race but was beaten by 11.9 lengths. His speed rating above does not match Just Bring It's. Garden Route is trained by. W Haggas and ridden by Ryan Moore. He is a classic false favourite. More about false favourites later.
Result.
The two finished clear of the rest with Just Bring It being the stronger in the finish despite Ryan Moore throwing the Kitchen Sink at Garden Route.
I always like to check why my selections won or lost. Watching replays can be highly informative. I recommend you watch as many replays as possible I use the Sporting Life site, but there are others. There is far more to ratings than meets the eye you really do need to study where the rating comes from. Beware of top-rated horses that won last time out and have taken a hike in official ratings. Also, horses that ran in a much higher-class race but were well beaten can sometimes earn a high Rating and Speed rating.

Ratings

On the 27th of September 2023 I looked at two races I thought it would be worth paying an interest in. They both had similar characteristics. The two races were the 2:30 at Goodwood, a 1M Hcp £15K Class 2 race, and the 4:25 at Redcar, a 1M2f Hcp £5K Class 4 race.

The first thing that caught my eye in these two races was the fact that Charlie Johnston had a runner in each race. I mention in the chapter on trainers how I like to check his runners. That situation will change soon too. On this occasion the fact that Charlie Johnston had a runner in each race and the fact that I have a good handle on how his horses fair in races currently it was a good starting point for the day.

I will take each point at a time and run through my thinking in each race in precise detail. I will start with the 2:30 at Goodwood, Charlie Johnston runner was The Gatekeeper. When first looking at his form the first thing I looked at was the number of times he had either won or been placed. I downloaded his form into a spreadsheet. If I take all his winning races to runners as shown below the average is six.

1st Musselburgh, Runners 4
1st Newcastle, Runners 7,
1st Newmarket, Runners 8
1st Goodwood, Runners 5

Average for his winning races is 6 runners.

He was also placed four times with the average for his placed and his winning races is 7.6 runners.

The average number of runners for all his races where he did not place is 14.7. As there are only 7 runners in today's race, I am quite keen to check this race out further. The Gatekeeper's forecast price is 5/1.

Ratings

I watched all the contestants previous two races on the Sporting Life replays. The Gatekeeper finished 14/15 last time out not given a challenging time when his chance had gone. He tends to run up with the pace if not make the running. There are two others in the race who also like to make the running. Though the Gatekeeper won his penultimate race he did in fact finish second, he won the race in the steward's room however the time was good.

I then turned my attention to the then favourite Lattam. Lattam has now gone up 8lb in the handicap since putting three good races in on the bounce. Last time out at Goodwood he made no show at all, he never looked like getting into the race. I could never support a horse that makes no show. No matter how much they are dropping in class my theory was that Lattam may just be at the top of his handicap mark.

I then watched the races of Rhoscolyn who was 3/1 at the time. Rhoscolyn finished 7/17 at Leopardstown. The race was run in quite a slow time. The winner Broadhurst came from last to first inside the last two furlongs. Rhoscolyn was running on really well against a field of decent horses. As the race was initially run slow the speed figures look poor. it was a sprint to the line from two furlongs out. Where Rhoscolyn was doing as well as any heading to the post. It really does pay you to check these races out and not rely just on form figures alone. In his penultimate race at Goodwood, he also finished very strongly to win by 1.3 lengths.

My concerns now are that the three front runners are going to burn themselves out vying for the lead and Rhoscolyn with his very strong finish is going to come at the death to win this.

I have therefore lost faith in The Gatekeeper even though I think he could be the best horse in the race. Once I have a doubt in my mind, I know I need to leave the race alone.

Ratings

I now turn my attention to the 2:25 at Redcar and Charlie Johnston's other horse that has caught my eye. Pillar of Hope ran a very decent race in a good time last time out at Beverley. After a strong gallop the hill at Beverley takes some getting. Pillar Of Hope stuck to his work well being beaten by 1.9 lengths. He has also dropped another 1lb in the official ratings. Today he is racing at a course that Should suit him well. Redcar is nice and flat unlike Beverley with a stiff uphill finish, he ran a fast time at Beverley. Now he has found his form this flat track is really going to be to his liking.

I was a little concerned that Mick Easterby's horse Casilli came in from 8/1 to 9/2 in one leap. I watched all her last three races but really could not see any justification for the confidence in her. Though coming from an Easterby yard, it is always a concern. The fact that she is a Mare I would be happy to side against her. She always seems to be knocking on the door, but has not won since July 2022 and in seven races despite being dropped in class she has never made any impression on the leaders in all her races.

I watched the races of all the other runners and the only one that impressed me was Havana Party. He won comfortably at Hamilton last time out. I did not think the form matched up to Pillar of Hope at Beverley. I really could not see Casilli getting into it unless she improved considerably.

Highway Grey, Tim Easterby's horse has run 14 times since his last win. Again, despite being dropped considerably in class he has never looked like winning. Charlie Johnston's horses are on fire after a slight lull. Pillar of Hope looks excellent value here for his 9/2 price tag.

The result of the 2:30 at Goodwood was that Rhoscolyn 7/2 won a tight finish running on past the three front runners very late. The Gatekeeper was a tiring 4th. He will get another chance in a small field when he has not got so much competition for the lead.

Ratings

My original assumption that The Gatekeeper was in a favourable position as he was in a small field was dashed after watching the races of all the runners and assuming as to how the race would be run.

In the 4:25 at Redcar Pillar of Hope did win his race by over three lengths quite comfortably.

I could not see that anything was likely to get to him was also correct.

Watching the races really does help. You should never rely on Speed Ratings or just Ratings alone though they are a good guide. Use them to see why a horse had a bad race or if he could have improved on its rating.

Another example of using ratings to good effect
3:50 Wolverhampton 25th May 2023
Class 4, £6K

This was a 5-runner race with a very hot favourite with an SP of 2/11 not a race I would look at normally. However, the red-hot favourite was under pressure to scrape home by half a length last time out.

HRB ratings for the race are copied in the table below. Again, a number of columns have been left out for clarity.

Wolverhampton 25th May 2023

Place	Horse	LR	2LR	Total	Odds
1st	Ottaman Prince (IRE)	79	34	167	2/11
4th	Zeno (FR)	58	32	135	17/2
2nd	Exorbitant	57	27	126	11/2
3rd	Buddys Beauty	27	13	60	200/1
5th	Hanover Girl79	0	0	2	66/1

Ratings

You can see in the Totals column that the favourite **Ottoman Prince** was rated well clear and duly won. However, that is not the interesting part of the table.

The one we are interested in is **Buddys Beauty** having her first run for over a year with a rating of 61 for this race. she finished third not far away splitting two horses rated 136 & 128. Therefore, Buddys Beauty rating for the race should be considerably better next time out.

Part of my notes on her trainer read "*2nd time out horses often improve particularly if racing in the rear.*"

The next time Buddys Beauty ran was in a Class 6, 4K race at Nottingham.

Nottingham
15th June 2023

Place	Horse	LR	2LR	TTL	Odds
4th	Spanish Angel (IRE)	63	27	137	6/4
2nd	Apache Star (IRE)	58	19	117	9/1
5th	Tilsworth Ony Ta	54	15	107	9/1
9th	Boarhunt	43	28	107	8/1
3rd	Hot Scoop	50	17	105	15/2
6th	Coleys Koko (IRE)	42	27	104	11/2
1st	Buddys Beauty (IRE)	61	12	99	20/1
7th	Suanni	41	16	91	15/2
8th	Trulie Good	31	14	69	40/1

Ratings

The figure I am interested in is her last race which is the third column in the table. You can see that it is out of line with her position in the overall final ratings. Her rating of 61 is remarkably close the warm favourites rating of 63. I believe the opposition she met last time was better than today's opposition. Plus, the fact from the comments on her trainer she is likely to improve today. She did of course oblige at 20/1. She then went on to win another Class 6 £4K race at Leicester at 7/2 winning comfortably. This time achieving a total rating of 134 close to where we thought she should have been after her come back race. Races like this with Form like this are hard to find but they are there every day.

Ratings alone are only a guide it is how you decide to use them that is crucial to your success. I like to use them in conjunction with trainer comments and trainers current form for their runners. There are literally hundreds of different ways to use ratings. There is no one right way it takes practice and homework. HRB ratings are as good as any I have ever come across. I am satisfied with the results that I get from them. Study them and find a niche. just remember Thoroughbred horses are not machines. They will not always perform the same every time they run. As an example, I have put a table together of HRB's top rated horse in each discipline for the last one thousand races.

The ratings produced have a particularly good Profit/Loss return though they are all slightly on the negative side. It would not take a genius to turn the returns into a profit by reducing the number of selections by a minimum of 50%.

You can see from the table on the following page that HRB have probably produced ratings for Flat racing. They do give you the option of producing ratings of your own by editing either theirs or your own produced ratings. If you are a ratings fan, go ahead and see what you can come up with.

Ratings

Disciplin	Top rated Win%	Top Rated Place%
UK Flat Hcps	23.33%	47.43%
UK Flat Non Hcps	31.01%	58.65%
Irish Flat Hcps	18.22%	42.93%
Irish Flat Non Hcps	30.12%	58.91%
UK AW Hcps	19.75%	47.86%
UK AW Non Hcps	30.24%	60.00%
Irish AW Hcps	16.43%	43.32%
Irish AW Non Hcps	31.25%	63.46%

HRB's top rated horse very nearly produce a profit in most disciplines, as I said it will not take a genius to narrow the top-rated horses down to show a profit. However, beware that they are only show what has happened in the past which is no guarantee that will happen in the future.

I just want to show you how useful ratings can be for the avid follower of ratings. I dare say several followers of HRB ratings would have noticed this.

One of the things I look for to find Value for Money selections is horses that finish outside the first four but finish close up to the winner. Particularly if the races were run in a relative fast time. The betting public and bookmakers overlook these horses . You can often get some real value from these horses.

In the 2:47 Ayr 03/10/23, A Class 4 £5K race. Hartswood was top rated by HRB see the table on the following page.

Ratings

Horse	Total	Odds	LR	2LR
Hartswood	171.2	8/1	78.1	35.1
Ayr Poet	155.7	5/1	59.7	38.9
Star Start	153.8	2/1	73.1	27.3
Bashful	151.3	17/2	63.9	24.4
Tilsitt	151.1	7/1	70.9	26.7
Montevideo	140.5	28/1	74.6	19.5
Stressfree	136.6	9/2	63.2	0.0
Glasses Up	134.2	8/1	57.1	24.8

You can see that Hartswood is 15+ points ahead of the rest there is nothing too unusual about that. Horses can be rated superior to the rest of the field it does not always mean they are the best in the race.

You then have four horses rated remarkably close to each other including Star Start the favourite. Stress Free has only had one race, so for a debutant that is quite a good rating. If you then checked the speed ratings, you would see that Hartswood is third in the list. His last race was 11 pts clear of all the rest. He was also clear of the rest in his penultimate race. Star Start the favourite was the bottom of the speed ratings in all its last four races.

Star Start won a class 6 £4K race last time out in fact he has only ever ran in class 6 races in his last ten starts. Hartswood last race was a class 4 £17K race he finished 5th beaten by 1.3Lengths. That was over 1Mile. If you watch the race, he took some getting going in the straight but when he did, he was catching the leader's hand over fist. Today's trip of 1m 2f will be ideal.

Ratings

The straight at Ayr is four furlongs this will play to his strengths should he take time to get going once again. Hartswoods's last race finishing 5th beaten by 1.3L, tells me there will be value in his price today. With the extra 2 Furlongs plus the long run in at Ayr, plus his last two speed figures and clear top rated by HRB, makes him a standout selection.

Result
1st Hartswood 8/1
2nd Stressfree 9/2
3rd Ayr Poet 5/1

Star Start the 2/1 favourite was 7th, you could have tackled this race in a number of ways. Laying the false favourite may have been one way. Backing Hartswood for a place would have been a decent bet too. At 8/1 with so much in his favour he really was a standout selection.

You do not get selections like this every day from ratings you need to check other factors too. Also, they are not going to jump out at you waving a flag. You need to do your homework and go looking for them.

Hartswood was one of five top rated winners at Ayr that day..

04/10/2023

The following day there was another standout selection, with the help of ratings.

3:42 Nottingham
Class 3 £9K 5f
Handicap

What caught my eye in this race was that the first two in the ratings table were rated well clear of the rest both in total ratings and their last race ratings.

Ratings

Horse	Total	Odds	LR	2LR
Spoof	196.9	9/4	101.1	26.6
Fantyasy Master	190.9	5/2	97.6	32.6
Desert Games (Ire)	176.1	17/2	83.0	38.1
Hiya Mate	167.1	15/2	60.3	35.9
Elegant Erin (Ire)	164.7	15/2	69.0	33.5
Angle Land	164	12/1	72.9	39.6
Sir Titus (Ire)	150.1	13/2	54.7	43.6

The ratings and the odds suggest that this is a two-horse race that is rarely the case. I thought it would be worth checking this race out further. I did check all the runners but let us concentrate on the first two in the ratings. You can see from the table below they both had similar form from their last race.

Spoof	Haydock	2/9<1L	5f	£31k	Cl2
Fantasy Master	Nottingham	2/10<1L	6f	£15k	Cl2

Spoof's last race was for £31k whereas Fantasy Masters last race was for £15k that normally does not mean a great deal. Let us look at the ratings for both in their last races.

To get a feel for the strength of a horses last race I would look at the Horses rating from top rated to bottom rated of each horse in their respective previous races.

Spoof, 205-142 : Fantasy Master, 184-95

Hiya Mate had stronger ratings from top to bottom, but he was beaten by 12+Lengths and that is a long way in 5f race.

Ratings

I then check the ratings where I bring all the competitor's ratings to 100% as I have mentioned earlier. Spoof went from 69 to 101. Fantasy Master went from 85 to 101 both have identical last race ratings.

Spoof has improved considerably more than Fantasy Master though they have both shown improvement. Also, Spoof was rated even higher in his third last race which shows he really does have ability.

I then check the trainer's current form.

Horse	Trainer	Annual average	Last 14 days	Place %
Spoof	Kevin Frost	7%	1/9- 11%	44%
Fantasy Master	Darryll Holland	10%	0/16 - 0%	31%

My notes on Kevin Frost ask me to check runners that are dropping in class Spoof is doing just that today. I am yet to find anything that suggests Fantasy Master is equal to spoof in this race. There are negatives around all the other runners.

Spoof won the race at 9/4 Fantasy Master was 4th

Not a great price but there was value in his price.

In the past I may have then searched all the other races for something that stands out. These days once I have found a runner like this. Why spend more time looking for something else. My time is better spent watching previous days racing looking for something that maybe good value in the future.

Ratings

06/10/2023

I have had a good week, so I did not intend picking anything out today. Just a day to relax and enjoy watching the racing or doing jobs around the house. However, after burning the midnight oil last night, I thought I would add a few more pages to this book.

Then a couple of things caught my eye when I flicked through the ratings for all the races.

Firstly, it looked like a day to leave alone as far as ratings were concerned. I looked at one race at Newcastle where a couple of trainers were traveling to Newcastle for the Evening racing. Not a thing they do lightly as it is a 241-mile trip one way. As all three were in the same race I left it alone and did not bother looking at the race again. As it turned out they finished 1st, 2nd, and 3rd at 8/1, 5/1 & 7/1 with Roger Varian's horse beating the two John Gosden runners.

The race that caught my eye was the 4:02 an Apprentice Race over 6 furlongs. I spent a considerable amount of time analysing this race. More than usual to be honest as it looked to be interesting. Generally, I leave apprentice races alone as a betting medium. However, they are useful for looking for useful claiming riders for the future.

The forecast favourite was South Dakota Sioux. I could see exactly why he would be favourite. Today's race is a Class 6 £3K race, South Dakota Sioux finished 4th in a Class 6 £3K race last time out. There are others in the race that ran in a Class 2 £18K race last time out. Now I am really interested in analysing the form for this race.

First, let me show you what caught my eye in the first place while looking through the ratings for this race.

Ratings

Both Kats Bob and After John the two top rated horses were both higher in the rating on their last race alone than the rest of the field. The reason for that is that they both ran in the Class 2 £18K race finishing 11th and 13th with hardly anything between them. Kats Bob today is 1lb better off. I watched the replay of this race many times. I concluded that Kats Bob was so unlucky in the race. Whereas After John who finished ahead of him was flat to the boards and may not improve on his rating. Kats Bob ran into a great deal of trouble and was snatched up on several occasions. Therefore, I was sure that Kats Bob had the beating of his stable companion After John.

I have shown on the following page the ratings when I bring all HRB ratings to 100%. I just want to point out again that HRB have a total of 20 Columns full of information. I am showing you a fraction of the information that could be looked at. I am just showing the name of the horse and their last race rating to make this point. they are in order of each horses total rating (Not Shown).

The other table is the speed rating for each horse also in order of their total rating.

You can see in the ratings 100% check working up from the bottom just as we did with Buddys Beauty earlier that South Dakota Sioux's rating is out of line with those around him. His last race rating must be an overall improvement compared with what he had done previously.

Also in the speed rating table working up from the bottom both South Dakota Sioux and Kats Bob rating are out of line with those around them.

Ratings

HRB Ratings Levelled to 100%

Horse	LR
Kats Bob	75.6
Saison Dor	69.9
Written Broadcast	64.0
Caribbean Sunset	34.7
After John	78.2
Moralisa	75.7
Lily In the Jungle	55.7
Pembrokeshire	37.2
South Dakota Sioux	71.3
Claim The Stars	59.3
Shotley Royale	39..9
Spartan Fighter	57.6

Speed Ratings

Horse	LR
Spartan Fighter	59.41
After John	76.81
Caribbean Sunset	43.08
Saison Dor	63.56
Claim The Stars	71.4
Pembrokeshire	52.97
Written Broadcast	62.3
Lily In the Jungle	59.56
Kats Bob	76.64
Moralisa	56.21
South Dakota Sioux	63.21
Shotley Royale	52.05

South Dakota Sioux has a quite high-speed rating for a class 6 £3k race. I thought I would check that in HRB's Advanced Results Search, sure enough it was a very fast run race better than some Class 4 races over the same distance at Newcastle. You really need to watch the race to see what I am talking about with South Dakota Sioux.

Ratings

The race was run on the 26th of September at Newcastle at 20:00 South Dakota Sioux reared leaving the stalls and was at the back of the field. In the last half furlong in this fast run race, he was coming through extremely well, when the jockey lost an iron got unbalanced and started to pull him up. Finishing fourth if that had not happened, he would have probably finished 2nd and got a better rating.

Also, you can see that Kats Bob has a rating out of line in his speed ratings too. To me this makes them both good value for money selections. Kats Bob opened in the market at 8/1 and quickly got backed in to 100/30 (Traders take note) South Dakota Sioux opened at 11/2 and stayed close to that throughout. Caribbean Sunset opened at 13/2 and got backed in to 5/2 favourite. The reason for that is anybody's guess the only reason I could think of is that he had a jockey on board that has done well at Newcastle in the past. Having watched his races where he has finished well behind Kats Bob, I could not see a reason for the flood of money.

Result
1st Kats Bob 4/1
2nd South Dakota Sioux 11/2
3rd Claim The Stars 20/1
4th Caribbean Sunset 5/2 Fav

Another John was sixth, Kats Bob and South Dakota Sioux fought out the finish clear of the rest. There was nothing about the race that told me it should turn out any differently. I will show other examples of looking at ratings from the bottom up just to clarify the point.

Ratings

The next race I looked at was the 5:45 at Newcastle a Class 4 £5k race over 1m. The reason I picked this race was first there are only eleven runners, I tend to look at handicaps from eight to eleven-runners. Secondly that the top horse on ratings was well above the rest last time out. I then used my ratings check which showed he was also way above the rest. I want to concentrate on speed ratings this time not just handicap ratings. There is a chapter on speed ratings later in the book. This race could come under any heading therefore I will use it here as the ratings are also important. That is how I noticed this horse in the first place.

The table below shows the speed ratings for the last three races of each horse plus its overall rating.

Horse	Rating	LR	2LR	3LR
Starshiba	75.07	85.74	65.72	72.64
Whitefeathersfall	73.69	63.51	67.34	80
Spirit Genie	73.53	71.05	57.29	80.56
Siam Fox	72.97	79.72	81.47	66.93
Tajawal	70.11	71.84	63.18	70.04
Miami Thunder	67.22	70.16	72.59	76.44
Archduke Ferdinand	66.4	64.69	65.76	50.69
Oh So Charming	65.59	63.52	68.86	50.46
Panning For Gold	64.08	78.44	63.78	65.56
Colourfull Dream	63	72.96	57.15	58
Cusak	59.56	65.27	62.12	49.13

Ratings

You can see in the table that Panning For Gold is third from bottom in Speed Ratings yet he is top by some margin in the ratings table. Again, let us look at the last race in the speed ratings highlighted on the previous page. Working from the bottom we can see that Panning For Gold is out of line with a rating of 78.44 there are four horses above him with lower ratings last time out.

The reason that Panning For Gold is way above the others in the ratings tables is because he has won five of his last six races. Consequently, he has gone up in the official ratings from fifty-two to a rating of seventy-seven today. Normally that should be enough to stop any horse continuing a winning sequence. If the trainer is smart enough and D M Simcock is just that, they can counteract the rise in official ratings by moving the horse up in class. part of my notes on D M Simcock read *"Watch for him moving horses up in class to carry less weight."*

Panning For Gold last race was in a Class 5 £4k race. Today he is in a Class 4 £5k race. His official rating last time was seventy today it has gone up yet another 7lb to seventy-seven. however last time out he carried 9-7 today despite the rise in official ratings he will only carry 9-3. He ran a fast time last time out as we can see from his rating so today with less weight, he can equal that time but maybe able to better it as he has less weight to carry.

If you check Panning For Gold's past history you will see that he won a Class 6 £3K race carrying 9-12, he then ran in a Class 5 £5K race carrying 9-4 and won again. He went up 5lb in the official ratings and failed to win next time out. He then ran off the same handicap mark and won again. Now he is up another 7lb but carrying less weight.

Ratingss

The table below shows all the horses in today's race and how their weight today compares with the weight they carried last time out.

Horse	+/- weight Difference	LR Speed Rating
Starshiba	+18	85.74
Whitefeathersfall	-11	63.51
Spirit Genie	+10	71.05
Siam Fox	+2	79.72
Tajawal	+3	71.84
Miami Thunder	+10	70.16
Archduke Ferdinand	=	64.69
Oh So Charming	+8	63.52
Panning For Gold	-4	78.44
Colourfull Dream	+18	72.96
Cusak	-9	65.27

Starshiba with the highest speed rating last time out is now carrying 18lb more than his last race which is enough to slow him up considerably here. Panning For Gold who has the next highest rating and is out of line in the table with his last rating is down 4lb, therefore could improve again. Whitefeathersfall is down 11lb but did not clock a decent speed last time. Cusak is down 9lb so could improve on his rating today. Tajawal who ended up as the 9/4 fav clocked a decent speed last time and now carries another 3lb, looking at the table horses like Oh So Charming 14/1, Miami Thunder 9/2, Colourful Dream 14/1, and Spirit Genie 40/1.

Ratings

are up against it today. Ironically, they all finished in the last four too. Panning For Gold won clear top on ratings, has the fastest speed figure and carrying less weight won the race at 5/1. Tajawal was 2nd at 9/4 fav, third was Cusak 11/1 who had a rating of 65 and now carries 9lb less.

I would not be surprised if D M Simcock does not raise Panning For Gold again in class just to lower the weight he will carry again.

Let us look at a race run on the 09/10/23 at Windsor a Class 5 £4K race. Looking at the market it is set up to be between just the top two in the market. Form wise I would agree with that. Therefore, I will just show a table with just those two runners.

Horse	Rating	Odds	L	2L
Midream	151.6	2/1	69	0
Silvretta	134.7	4/6	63.7	29

Silvretta has has had three races and Midream just one. Part of my notes on A M Balding Silvretta's trainer read *"Horses can improve after an initial race"* and sure enough Silvretta did for her next two races.

Part of my Notes for Midream's trainer read, *"It does not matter where his 2yo's finish first time out they show big improvement in their next race."*

If we look at the form of Silvretta in her last two races she was "headed final Strides" and "Weakened" not positive comments and watching her races that is exactly what she did. Midream's comments end in "Stayed on one pace inside final furlong" from the trainer comments we know that Midream will improve. She is already above Silvretta's ratings in their respective last races.

Ratings

I then looked at the Speed Figures for the two, copied below..

Horse	Rating	Odds	L	2L
Silvretta	68.64	4/6	67.63	73.98
Midream	68.41	2/1	68.41	0

Midream is so close to Silvretta with improvement that will inevitably happen she would clearly be my favourite to come out on top in this contest.

Result

1st Midream 2/1

2nd Silvretta 4/6

Again Silvretta was one paced in the final furlong. Going on Ratings and Speed Figures Midream was a decent investment. You still need to do your homework by watching the races though.

How can we find the bigger priced selections that are likely to give us a good run for our money by using ratings. If you are a regular HRB user, you may already do this. If you are not, I recommend that you check this out at some point. it is a little time consuming, but the results can be very worthwhile. If you do not use Horseracebase at all and you are into your racing in big way. You really are missing an absolute massive amount of information that is at your fingertips.

One of the things that I do to find selections that others may not be looking at is to pull up the ratings for each race. Look for a horse close to the bottom of the ratings that has a rating in its last race very close to either the top-rated horse or the favourite.

On the following page I have reprinted the ratings from the 4:20 race at Chelmsford on 14th October 2023.

Ratings

4.20 Chelmsford City (7 runners)
Chelmsford City Racecourse Membership Nursery
1m2f (2200 yards)
Class 6, Standard, 2yo, Win: £4004

Horse	Total	Odds	LR	2LR
Tasmanian Legend (IRE)	135.0	4/1	58.7	26.4
Made In China (IRE)	118.1	Evens	60.1	21.2
Royal Hussar (IRE)	111.0	8/1	43.2	30.3
Unleash Hell (IRE)	110.1	12/1	48.7	26.6
Free Speech (IRE)	101.1	9/1	52.3	20.1
Catena (IRE)	99.4	50/1	37.3	18.8
Dubai Venture (IRE)	99.2	17/2	48.8	17.8

You will know by now that I place a great deal of importance on the horses most recent race. In the race ratings above the highlighted column is each horse's rating from their last race. Looking at Free Speech's last rating you can see that it is slightly out of line with others around her. On its own just looking at these ratings there is nothing startling.

Free Speech is not close enough to the favourite Made In China to take a second look. As I have said before I have a set of ratings where I bring all the runner's previous ratings up to 100%. To do this you just need to go to the Ratings Machine V2/ Horse Score/Timeline/Runs Ago Score and change the last ten races to 100% and that is it, simple.

Ratings

Spotting Free Speech here out of line with the Total ratings. I then just run my ratings check which is just one click away. My 100% ratings are printed below.

Horse	Total	Odds	LR	2LR
Unleash Hell (IRE)	280.1	12/1	69.2	75.8
Tasmanian Legend (IRE)	278.9	4/1	63.4	68.3
Royal Hussar (IRE)	255.1	8/1	61.6	79.2
Free Speech (IRE)	240.1	9/1	75.5	68.9
Catena (IRE)	239.5	50/1	47.1	67.6
Made In China (IRE)	235.0	Evens	75	67.7
Dubai Venture (IRE)	213.4	17/2	63	55.8

Now things have changed very much in favour of Free Speech. Her Last Race rating is now higher than all the other runners last race ratings. At this point you can ignore the total ratings as they are the total of the last four races. I am only interested in the last race this does not on its own make Free Speech a decent selection. You need to look at other factors for the other runners particularly an Even money favourite.
Made In China is trained by Charlie Johnston, a trainer I have plenty of respect for as you will read in the trainer's section. His last race was in a Class 6 £3K race. You can gloss it up as much as you like. The facts are it was a low-class race, and he was beaten into 4th starting the 7/2 favourite. He had been dropped from a class 5 £4K race and as you will read later Charlie Johnston's horses when dropped in class need a good looking at again today, he is contesting a Class 6 race.

Ratings

Made In China's failure to capitalise on his previous drop in class for Charlie Johnston tells me that Class 6 is his level at this current time.

The next thing I would do is have a quick look at the speed figures for the race printed below.

Horse	Rating	Odds	L	2L
Tasmanian Legend (IRE)	69.2	4/1	53.45	55.51
Royal Hussar (IRE)	64.97	8/1	55.95	66.7
Dubai Venture (IRE)	63.45	17/2	65.08	56.17
Made In China (IRE)	58.07	Evens	58.59	60.91
Catena (IRE)	58.04	50/1	44.3	45.3
Unleash Hell (IRE)	57.79	12/1	56.94	60.23
Free Speech (IRE)	58.16	9/1	58.16	55.25

Free Speech is now the bottom of the table on overall speed ratings however her last race is almost equal to the favourites last race. Only Dubai Venture has a higher rating.

From what I know about Charlie Johnston I have already made my mind up that Made In China's Even money price is absurd. None of this is making Free Speech an automatic selection it is making her very interesting indeed.

Looking at Free Speech's form and my notes on her trainer is what makes her look more than just very interesting. Part of my notes on her trainer read *"After 3 Maiden races horses can show improvement for their first Handicap or Nursery race"* Free Speech has had 3 races in Maiden company. Another part of my notes on her trainer read *"If held up in the rear can improve quite a bit next time out"* Free Speech's race notes for her 3 Maiden races read like this.

Ratings

LR: Held up in Mid division.
2LR: In Touch in Rear.
3LR: Always towards Rear,

Today Free Speech is dropped in class for her first race in a
Nursery.
Her last race rating and her last race speed figure give her a very
good chance against the Charlie Johnston horse. I believe she will
now be fully race fit for this contest. The result was.

1st: Free Speech 9/1
2nd: Tasmanian Legend 4/1
3rd: Unleash Hell 12/1
4th: Made In China Evens (Fav)

In this race Free Speech was certainly worth taking a chance with
at 9/1. Made In China would have been worth laying at that very
restrictive price. Not that I am into laying horses but a few of my
friends are.
These sorts of races take quite a bit of searching for, you then need
to evaluate all the runners not just those that have caught your eye
because a high rating. The notes you keep on trainers provided you
keep them up to date are an extremely powerful help to finding
runners that are likely to run a big race at a big price.
There will be times when the form of horses gets intermingled and it
is difficult to separate them. The answer to that is simple, just leave
the race alone. I usually like more than one reason for supporting a
horse and making an investment, in the case of Free Speech I had
four reasons, Ratings, Trainer's comments, form of her previous
races and no confidence in the favourite.
On the following page is another example where the trainers
comments were valuable in assessing the chances of the runners.

Ratings

Tue 24th Oct 2023

8.00 Wolverhampton (8 runners)

Always Gamble Responsibly With BetUK Handicap

5f (1121 yards)

Class 6, Standard, 3yo+, Win: £3140

I could have put this race under any heading Ratings, Trainers, Speed Figures maybe it sits better here. First, let us look at the ratings for the race copied from HRB below.

Horse	Total	Odds	LR	2LR
Bankrupt (IRE)	143.6	8/1	77.4	21.1
Nordic Glory (IRE)	134.7	4/1	75.1	25.4
Stay Smart	117.2	100/30	47.5	21.6
Urban Dandy (IRE)	113.3	9/2	55.9	15.7
Mucky Mulconry (IRE)	110.3	6/1	38	24.1
Close Of Play	107.5	40/1	62	14.5
Gustav Graves	104.1	4/1	42	16.8
Mutabaahy (IRE)	92.4	16/1	38	17.9

Stay Smart is the 100/30 Favourite part of my notes on Stay Smart's trainer read *"Horses always need a run after a break"* Stay Smart has had 117 days off the course to me that constitutes a significant break. Also, his HRB rating is for his last race is thirty points behind the top horse. Gustav Graves is in my list of horses whose stallions prodigy are in the low end of the table when racing in five furlong races. Therefore, I would automatically discount him. Also, he has had twenty-nine races over five furlongs and only won once. He is also thirty-five points behind the top of the table in their last race ratings. That is five good reasons to look elsewhere other than the favourite two.

Ratings

The two top horses in the ratings and in their last race ratings are clear of the rest of the field. Below I have printed my 100% ratings.

Horse	Total	Odds	LR	2LR
Bankrupt (IRE)	304.4	8/1	88.9	51.6
Stay Smart	283	100/30	61.5	64.6
Gustav Graves	280.3	4/1	57	51.6
Nordic Glory (IRE)	275.4	4/1	88	70.9
Mucky Mulconry (IRE)	266.3	6/1	43.9	62.4
Urban Dandy (IRE)	242.2	9/2	67.1	21.3
Mutabaahy (IRE)	218.3	16/1	56.5	54.4
Close Of Play	142.4	40/1	72.1	17.5

Again, two horses stand out on their last race. Bankrupt and Nordic Glory. They also both showed improvement from their second last race.

Below are the speed ratings for the race.

Horse	Rating	L	2L
Stay Smart	69.62	60.04	65.24
Nordic Glory (IRE)	69.07	66.8	66.27
Mutabaahy (IRE)	68.32	57.04	56.95
Gustav Graves	64.9	50.84	58.8
Urban Dandy (IRE)	62.3	58.76	42.92
Mucky Mulconry (IRE)	59.85	56.96	58.92
Bankrupt (IRE)	58.86	60.92	53.68
Close Of Play	57.73	62.12	36.12

Ratings

Now Nordic Glory has the best rating last time out. Bankrupt is next if we do not count the 40/1 outsider a filly whose time for her last race does not look correct as none of the contestants had done anything like that speed previously. Bankrupt's speed Rating improved more than Nordic Glory between their second last and last rating.

We have negatives about two at the head of the market and positives about two of the others

Result
1st Bankrupt 8/1
2nd Nordic Glory 4/1
3rd Stay Smart 4/1

It was difficult to split Bankrupt and Nordic Glory and so it turned out there was only a Head between them at the line.

It was the negatives about the two at the head of the market that drew my attention to this race not any positives or the ratings, I may have sat the day out if I had not spotted that the two with negative comments were at the head of the market and had poor ratings.

They were both false favourites.

Before we go any further it does not always work out as simple as this. It may have turned out that something else in the race sprouted new legs. Or one of my two did not get the run of the race. Ratings, Speed Ratings and your trainer comments plus losing systems are all guides to help you. Watching the races is also a guide you still need to invest sensibly to make sure you come out on top overall. Always bare in mind that horses are not machines, what you are trying to do is get value for your investments, value could be Even Money or twenty-five to one.

Ratings

The previous races all worked out very nicely maybe I made it sound too simple. It does not always work out like that by looking for ratings that are out of line with the others around them. Or starting from the bottom to the top. Let us look at two races where it does not work out so well and see if we can see why that is. You should always do this if your selections flop there may be a particularly good reason for it. Something that you may have missed in your form study or your selection just had an off day or did not get the rub of the green during the race.

I checked both races as the horses in question looked on the face of things exactly like the previous selections. The first race is the 4:15 at Lingfield on the 26th of October 2023, Ratings for the race copied below.

Horse	Rating	L	2L
Red Hat Eagle	148	76	31
Goldsmith (IRE)	143	64	31
Al Hargah (IRE)	125	54	20
Showlan Spirit	106	48	29
Mykonos St John	100	39	25
Pierce (IRE)	98	42	18
Tribal Wisdom (IRE)	96	43	17
Hurricane Kiko (IRE)	90	34	16
Tiz Likely (IRE)	88	52	12
The Game Is Up	86	45	12

Starting from the bottom of the participants last race one horse stands out Tiz Likely with a rating of 52 has five runners above him with a lower rating. I have printed on the following page my 100% ratings.

Ratings

Remember on the previous page you are looking at the rating for the horses last race, compared to their position sorted by the Total Rating column.

Horse	LR	2LR	3LR	4LR
Goldsmith (IRE)	81	85	81	78
Red Hat Eagle	86	82	74	77
Al Hargah (IRE)	69	56	75	92
Mykonos St John	60	71	69	65
Showlan Spirit	70	73	53	45
Tribal Wisdom (IRE)	59	29	67	48
Hurrican Kiko (IRE)	18	37	79	63
The Game Is Up	73	18	72	31
Pierce (IRE)	24	29	55	64
Tiz Likely (IRE)	73	17	25	39

Above we show the last four races of all horses with ratings levelled out to 100%. Now Tiz Likely is the bottom of all the ratings but still with a very good rating last time out. He also shows up well on speed ratings too. Therefore, you may think he is still a suitable selection you still need to do more checking.

Previously Tiz Likely has had 7 races prior to his last race which produced the good rating. The closest he got to the winner was 8.3 Lengths back in March. He finished last in five of those seven races. If we look at all Tiz Likely's Ratings in comparison to the other runners he has the worst rating in every single case bar the 4th last where The Game Is Up has one rating slightly worse. There is no reason that Tiz Likely improved that much last time out. He got a decent rating because the others in his last race had done better previously and dragged his rating up.

Ratings

When looking at ratings this way for example from the bottom up. Always check out why a horse has suddenly got an exceptional rating in comparison to all their previous races. It is likely it was not deserved. Ratings are produced from sets of data that have no feelings behind them. They are cold hard facts of horses and their previous races and the competition in them. If the race was run slowly or there was bumping in the race or something broke from the stalls very slow none of this can be picked up by data. As this race turned out Tiz Likely finished plumb last once again. Make a comment about his previous race that the ratings for the race may be too high, it may help you if the participants come up in another race with a high rating.

The next race we need to look at is on the same day 26th October 2023 the 7:00 at Wolverhampton, ratings copied below.

Horse	Rating	L	2L
Moon Flight (IRE)	144	69	26
Bright (IRE)	135	65	29
Kaidu (IRE)	132	59	33
Captain Bentley	122	73	16
Darkened Edge	124	62	23
Rooska (GER)	121	51	29
Advantag (IRE)	121	57	0
Almavillalobas	83	39	17

In this race we have a horse halfway up the table with a rating that is above anything else in the race. Often these are well worth looking at so let us dig a bit deeper into Captain Bentley.

My 100% ratings are on the following page.

Ratings

With the Leveller ratings below Captain Bentley is still close to the top-rated horse last time out.

What should set alarm bells ringing is where he comes in the overall table. second from bottom.

Horse	LR	2LR	3LR	4LR
Moon Flight (IRE)	79	60	76	82
Rooska (GER)	56	78	73	0
Bright (IRE)	72	71	55	0
Kaidu (IRE)	71	77	42	0
Darkened Edge	60	59	0	0
Advantage (IRE)	49	0	0	0
Captain Bentley	77	26	19	0
Almavillalobas	19	33	0	0

Prior to his decent rating Captain Bentley had only had two races. Just like Tiz Likely he finished last on both occasions. He then finished second in an extremely poor class 5 race. A race that the contestants would struggle in any Class 6 race. You can tell that by the ratings for the race. Because it was a class 5 race, they automatically get a higher rating. Again, you can see that Captain Bentley's second last and third last ratings are very poor.

Captain Bentley also finished last in this race. Again, you should make a note on the race where he obtained a good rating to remind yourself that the ratings produced are too high for the relative class of the horses.

Ratings produced by HRB are brilliant they allow you to check back as far as you like as to where winning form comes from. You cannot take ratings blindly. Always check and check again. It will pay you to miss races rather than invest blindly.

Ratings

Having had Covid for the last few days I have been having time off from looking for potential investments. I have booked my tickets for the November Handicap at Doncaster on November 11th now I am sitting with my feet up.

What I do at times like this when we have had heavy rain for the last few weeks and things on the flat racing courses are beginning to wind down. I find that looking through the days racing not to see why horses won certain races. But why did some favourites not perform as well as expected? If they had good ratings and good speed ratings etc but flopped, why did they?

Quite a lot of the time it is difficult to answer. It is just that horses are not machines. Sometimes you find that the ratings they achieved were just not warranted. That may go back several races.

Ratings are produced by known data. One good rating like we mentioned earlier with Tiz Likely and Captain Bentley is likely to stick with them. With the aforementioned two I will make a note on the races that gave them the good rating and check when horses from the same race run again. I would expect them to get a decent rating too. I would also expect them not to run as well as expected which would give me an edge in the race. I may or may not find something else in the race, but I would keep monitoring the situation until the form of the runners got so intermingled it would not pay to spend the time to follow that particular race. In the meantime, there will be numerous other races to look at.

You will never cover the whole spectrum of races such as the Flat, All Weather and National Hunt for both the UK and Ireland. There would be far too much data to analyse and keep up with. It would pay for you to specialise and stick to your favourite area of racing, that will also increase your enjoyment and possibly your profit.

Trainers

Introduction to trainers and why you should keep notes and constantly check them at regular intervals.

Trainers

One of the great things about HRB is the ability to make and keep notes. You can make notes on Horses, Jockeys, Trainers, Races and Stallions. These notes can appear "if you select them" next to the horses on the race card. I used to do this quite a bit in 2017-2018, these days I do not make so many notes on observations I have made on horses just getting lazier as I get older, I suppose. Believe me they are unbelievably valuable if you know what you are looking at.

In the back of the book there is a copy of some of the notes I made against some horses back in the day just to give you a flavour of what can be achieved.

However, one of the key areas for keeping notes for me is on trainers. This can be a rich sauce of information. Though this can vary as Trainers can be creatures of habit, they tend to use the same approach often with horses in their care. Also, you may be able to dismiss certain runners depending on the notes you have kept, as we demonstrated earlier.

By the time this book goes to print my notes on Trainers will have changed several times depending on each trainer's recent performance.

On the fifteenth June 2023, Ed Walker was running a well-built 2yo named Crack Shot, my notes for Ed Walker at the time read *"It does not matter where Ed's 2yo or 3yo finish 1st time out they show big improvement on in their second race"* Crack Shot ran in a class 4 £6K race first time out. I watched his previous race; Crack Shot is a well-built gelding he may need a race to get fully wound up. This time he is in a class 5 £4K race with little opposition of note. The amazing thing is Crack Shot was priced at 50/1 he remained at 50/1 up to an hour and half before the race he was then backed down to 18/1 and duly obliged. Betfair SP was 28.82. I helped myself to the 50/1 and backed it Each Way, this was purely down to notes kept on trainers.

Trainers

On another card the same day Amy Murphy was running Baileys Derbyday at Worcester. My notes at the time for Amy Murphy read. "*Watch for a change of head Gear, Amy knows her stuff when it comes to headgear*" again not in a strong race. Bailys Derbyday was wearing a Hood for the very first time, again duly obliged at 12/1. 18.41 on Betfair.

You can see that studying trainer's habits can pay very rewarding dividends. Of course, it does not work out all the time some races you will have notes on all the trainers. You need to to sort the wheat from the chaff that is extremely easy to do with Horseracebase very quickly too.

Keeping notes on trainers is something that little if any betting shop punters do. Only a very few professionals do. You will need to keep checking and re-checking your notes to make sure that what once was a habit still is. Do not forget that a trainer's string of horses can have difficulties too. That information is also readily available on Horseracebase.

8th August 2023

My notes on Miss L.A Perratt read" *Applies her trade mainly in Scotland, watch her horses when traveling South*". She had one runner entered at Chelmsford a 389-mile one way journey. She has only ever had two runners there previously back in 2008. Both placed at decent prices. Her one runner on this date Nasca duly obliged at 22/1 opened at 33/1.

On the same day, my Notes on G A Harker read "*Seems to have the patience to keep running horses until they have dropped down the OR then win, if finishing 2nd win next time*" His horse Rum Runner finished second then finished second another twice at good prices. The Official Rating did not change he then obliged at 10/1.

Of course patience is needed to find selections like these they do not all win but when they do it is extremely rewarding.

Trainers

My notes on Charlie Johnston who has recently taken over from his father Mark read "*A drop-in class and prize Money is very significant*". In fact, you can check this out on Horseracebase by going to Compare LR (Compare Last Race) if you click (less class) and (Less Prize Money.) You will see that his horses have made a profit on Betfair and at SP. Something very few other trainers achieve. He also shows a profit with the same scenario on the All Weather though very slight profit on Betfair. At the time of writing, he had one runner today that matched those credentials Sayidh Kingman who duly obliged at 9/2. Yesterday 08/08/2023 he had one runner that matched those credentials Wadacre Gomez who also obliged at 11/2, 7.9 at Betfair SP. Though these are excellent results currently they only land 19% of the time. Therefore,there are losing runs to negotiate just like any system. A copy of Charlie Johnston's winning and losing runs when dropped in class or prize money are copied from Horseracebase below.

Losing Sequences		Winning Sequences		Place Losing Seq		Place Winning Seq	
Sequence	Occurences	Sequence	Occurences	Sequence	Occurences	Sequence	Occurences
1	4	1	19	1	15	1	22
2	3	2	6	2	9	2	13
3	2			3	3	3	2
4	2			4	3	4	1
5	3			5	1		
6	2			6	3		
7	1			7	1		
8	1			8	1		
9	2			13	1		
10	1						
11	1						
13	1						
14	1						

Trainers

Though I have put the place results in the previous table it does not pay to back these horses to place. Place betting is another thing altogether. This book concentrates on win bets with a splattering of place advice only.

18/08/2023 Charlie Johnston had three runners matching the above credentials.

3:25 Wolverhampton: World without Love 4th 12/1

4:53 Thirsk: Quintus Maximus 3rd 17/2

6:20 Newmarket: True Wisdom 1st 33/1

19/08/2023 Another three runners today that match that same criteria.

3:10 Newmarket: Lincoln Legacy 1st 5/1

4:20 Newmarket: Blue Universe 3rd 6/1

3:50 Ripon: Spirit Catcher 1st 4/1

Of course, you also must balance Trainer selections with other runners in the race. You may find you have positive comments about 3 or 4 trainers in the same race. Unless you can weed their runners out by other means of form selection, I suggest you leave those races alone just enjoy the race.

Following trainer's methods as I have shown here can be very profitable indeed however a word of warning. This will not last. People will get wise the value will go. Charlie Johnston will highly likely change his training methods as time goes on but there will always be hundreds of other methods to look at. You just have to keep updating your comments and methods.

I update my trainer comments regularly, for the top trainers that have many runners I may check them three times per season. Smaller trainers I will update at least twice a season. Sometimes there is no need to change the comments, other times I would re-write a whole paragraph.

Trainers

2.15 Ffos Las (9 runners)

City Energy / EBF Novice Stakes (GBB Race)
7½f (1620 yards +32 yards rails adjustment)
Class 5, Good To Soft, 2yo, Win: £3564
Avg OR : 0, Median OR : 0
Left Handed, Stall Positioning : Outside

	Form	Horse	Trainer	Odds	HRB
	3	Go Daddy (IRE)	Muir, W R & Grassick, C	11/4	180
	3	I Love Paris (IRE)	Walker, Ed	7/2	174
	3	Going The Distance (IRE)	Beckett, R M	7/2	198
	4	Savvy Warrior (IRE)	Woods, S P C	5/1	172
	6	Break The Bank	Balding, A M	6/1	170
	none	Hand Of God	Charlton, Roger/Harry	14/1	42
	0	Speeding Bullet (IRE)	Hannon (Jnr), Richard	22/1	135
	9	Yellow Pages (IRE)	Watson, Archie	66/1	133
	7	Bree Anna Poppy	Evans, P D	150/1	115

The race above was run on the 25th of August 2023. I decided to concentrate on the first four in the betting as they were the most likely area the winner was going to come from. There is minor difference in the form of the four horses they all ran in a class four race last time out and showed up fairly well.

Trainers

Horseracebase rates Going the Distance the highest. As can be seen from the right-hand column. This suggests that he was the strongest of the four runners. looking back on each of their races and the ratings of the competitors I would agree with that, however that information alone does not substantiate a selection. I checked whether the trainer's horses are in particularly good form or are they running at their average for the year or below average.

The following screen shots from Horseracebase's trainers records tell a very interesting story.

	Days	Runners	Wins	Win P/L	Win%	Place	Place%
	7	10	0	-10	0%	2	20%
	14	20	1	-17.8	5%	5	25%
Go Daddy	30	33	2	-22.8	6%	9	27%
WR Muir	60	61	6	-31.3	10%	17	28%
	90	84	7	-49.8	8%	21	25%
	180	113	13	-23.3	12%	29	26%
	365	216	20	-78.47	9%	60	28%

	Days	Runners	Wins	Win P/L	Win%	Place	Place%
	7	29	8	4.24	28%	15	52%
	14	54	17	17.98	31%	28	52%
Going The Distance	30	119	35	34.69	29%	65	55%
R M Beckett	60	197	52	17.86	26%	103	52%
	90	275	62	-0.39	23%	131	48%
	180	390	88	-1.09	23%	183	47%
	365	649	124	-43.28	19%	271	42%

Setting the tables out like this you can see at glance which trainer's horses are in form and which are not. Also, which are running averagely well. WR Muir has only had one winner in his last twenty runners that was a 6/5 favourite here at Ffos Las.

	Days	Runners	Wins	Win P/L	Win%	Place	Place%
	7	18	1	-11.5	6%	3	17%
	14	34	5	-10.42	15%	9	26%
I Love Paris	30	71	14	-3.93	20%	24	34%
Ed Walker	60	135	25	1.65	19%	49	36%
	90	197	35	8.65	18%	72	37%
	180	293	44	37.15	15%	103	35%
	365	470	62	-45.99	13%	161	34%

	Days	Runners	Wins	Win P/L	Win%	Place	Place%
	7	11	0	-11	0%	1	9%
	14	21	0	-21	0%	4	19%
Savvy Warrior	30	42	4	11.5	10%	10	24%
S P Woods	60	75	8	3.5	11%	20	27%
	90	115	11	-16	10%	32	28%
	180	184	20	-37.83	11%	54	29%
	365	257	26	77.08	10%	84	33%

R M Beckett has had fifty-four runners in the last fourteen days
with a win percentage of 31%. Ed Walker's horses are as always
running well 15% in the last fourteen days. S P Woods horses are
not doing so well as he has had no winners and only four placed
horses in the last fourteen days. well below his average for the
year. Another point to note is that R M Beckett won this race last
year. Though I do not normally give credit to that, it is worth
noting. Going the Distance went on to win at 7/2. Though the
price is short the selection did stand out. You were always going
to get a good run for your money. R M Becket had another two
winners on the card at 4/5 and 15/2 plus a winner at Newmarket
too showing the well-being of his horses at this time.

Trainers

Other examples of looking at trainer's horses in form are given below. You can see from MP Tregoning's form figures his yearly average is 10%. in the last fourteen days his runners are running at 33%. In the last three days he has had one winner at 10/1 and a second at 12/1.

Recent Form By Days (All Races)

	Days	Runners	Wins	Win P/L	Win%	Place	Place%
	7	4	1	7	25%	2	50%
	14	6	2	15	33%	3	50%
	30	14	2	7	14%	5	36%
M.P. Tregoning	60	32	4	43.25	13%	8	25%
	90	47	4	28.25	9%	11	23%
	180	65	7	43.25	11%	19	29%
	365	123	12	13.58	10%	35	28%

Roger & Harry Charlton yearly average runs at 15%, last fourteen days they have had six winners from twenty runners 30% the last seven days have produced three winners at 9/4, 9/4, and 33/1.

Recent Form By Days (All Races)

	Days	Runners	Wins	Win P/L	Win%	Place	Place%
	7	10	3	1	30%	4	40%
	14	20	6	30.66	30%	8	40%
	30	33	9	30.16	27%	15	45%
Roger Charlton	60	63	16	55.67	25%	27	43%
	90	102	24	52.9	24%	42	41%
	180	149	26	10.81	17%	57	38%
	365	271	41	-40.61	15%	101	37%

George Scott

A trainer well worth looking at his runners as they can run up a sequence of wins. His runners generally run at 16%-win rate year upon year he currently has 22% winners in the last fourteen and thirty days. Today he had one horse at Hamilton where he has a 60%-win rate he trotted up at 2/1.

Trainers

Again, all that information is at your fingertips In Horseracebase you just need to do your homework.

Recent Form By Days (All Races)

	Days	Runners	Wins	Win P/L	Win%	Place	Place%
	7	2	1	1	50%	1	50%
	14	9	2	-3.8	22%	2	22%
	30	27	6	-3.07	22%	9	33%
George Scott	60	54	14	21.3	26%	23	43%
	90	83	15	0.3	18%	31	37%
	180	143	24	-6.2	17%	47	33%
	365	230	36	-38.33	16%	85	37%

Jack Jones

You can clearly see below that Jack Jones's horses have been improving over the last 90 days. His last three runners have produced 2 winners both at 100/30 and a second placed horse at 11/1 his placed horses are running at 71% so you are getting a good run for your money. His horses will be well worth following until the bubble bursts.

Recent Form By Days (All Races)

	Days	Runners	Wins	Win P/L	Win%	Place	Place%
	7	3	2	5.66	67%	3	100%
	14	7	3	4.91	43%	5	71%
	30	10	3	1.91	30%	7	70%
Jack Jones	60	20	6	9.66	30%	10	50%
	90	30	7	2.91	23%	14	47%
	180	62	13	17.21	21%	27	44%
	365	91	15	13.21	16%	34	37%

Trainers

Still sticking with the theme of trainers last night I was evaluating the form of runners in the 1:30 at Goodwood. You can see from the table below that Betties Bay ended up Favourite also she was top rated only slightly by HRB. Again, the race looks to be between first three in the market the following page evaluates my thinking on the race.

	Form	Horse	Trainer	Odds	HRB
	201	Betties Bay	Nicholls, Georgina	9/4	209
	725	Al Hujaija (IRE)	Varian, Roger	5/2	208
	5221	Adaay In Devon	Millman, B R	9/2	201
	5	Tayala	Walker, Ed	5/1	168
	4	Ruling Sovereign (IRE)	Scott, George	13/2	192
	42	Toosha (IRE)	Butler, John	20/1	175
	0	Invincible Siam (IRE)	Boughey, George	66/1	133

Trainers

Before **Betties Bay** won a CL4 £6K race at Newbury she ran in a Gr2 £65K race at Ascot on the face of it that is good form coming into this CL4 £8K race.

Al Hujaija ran in a CL2 £16K race at Newmarket beaten by 8.3 lengths again this is decent form in the terms of this race.

Adaay in Devon had won a CL5 £4K race at Windsor a race I expected him to win easily which he did in very commanding fashion.

Each of the trainer's current form is shown below.

Recent Form By Days (All Races)

	Days	Runners	Wins	Win P/L	Win%	Place	Place%
	7	0		0			
	14	0		0			
Georgina Nicholls	30	0		0			
Betties Bay	60	4	1	2.5	25%	1	25%
	90	9	1	-2.5	11%	2	22%
	180	14	1	-7.5	7%	4	29%
	365	14	1	-7.5	7%	4	29%

Recent Form By Days (All Races)

	Days	Runners	Wins	Win P/L	Win%	Place	Place%
	7	14	4	8.21	29%	7	50%
	14	38	11	11.31	29%	19	50%
Roger Varian	30	83	18	20.39	22%	37	45%
Al Hujaija	60	160	31	-5.32	19%	74	46%
	90	268	48	-31.88	18%	113	42%
	180	398	64	-100.88	16%	163	41%
	365	671	126	-101.51	19%	275	41%

Trainers

Recent Form By Days (All Races)

	Days	Runners	Wins	Win P/L	Win%	Place	Place%
	7	7	0	-7	0%	1	14%
	14	14	1	-9	7%	4	29%
B R Millman	30	35	6	-6.5	17%	11	31%
Adaay in Devon	60	67	9	-8.5	13%	21	31%
	90	102	13	-26.83	13%	32	31%
	180	192	26	-42.78	14%	66	34%
	365	319	41	-70.27	13%	112	35%

On the pure form figures it looks like the best trainer form is Georgina Nicholls and Roger Varian. However, we need to look past the percentage figures Georgina's winner was her only winner this year, she has had very few runners from her small string though she has had couple of decent seconds. I prefer to know more about her abilities to turn horses out to compete in this quite competitive race. We can see that Roger Varian's horses are doing Extremely well 29% in the last 14 days 10% up on his yearly average. B R Millman's figures do not look good do they 7% in the last 14 days and none of his last seven runners have won. Horseracebase gives a breakdown of the last two hundred runners of every trainer. When I checked B R Millman's results most of his last seven runners were outsiders. Starting at prices like 150/1, 22/1 25/1 with the shortest price being 13/2. I checked his horses that started at prices between 6/4 and 9/2 for the whole of 2023 and found that they make profit at SP. I then checked the breakdown of Handicap and Non-Handicap races surprisingly he has only had 8 non-handicap runners that have started between those two prices resulting in 50% winners. Showing a nice profit at SP.

Trainers

I compared that to Roger Varian who has had forty-one non-handicappers between those two prices with only 6 winners 14.63% showing a loss even on the exchanges.

Next, I checked the speed figures for the three horses, the table is shown below. You can see that Adaay in Devon was actually quicker according to the ratings than the other two.

Horse	Rating	Odds	L	2L	3L	4L
Betties Bay	72.28	9/4	68.92	72.31	75.61	0
Al Hujaija (IRE)	67.29	5/2	68.29	74.08	39.12	0
Toosha (IRE)	65.44	20/1	70.48	55.36	0	0
Adaay In Devon	65.37	9/2	71.64	61.48	64.27	60.76
Ruling Sovereign (IRE)	65.15	13/2	65.15	0	0	0
Tayala	65.01	5/1	65.01	0	0	0
Invincible Siam (IRE)	55.52	66/1	55.52	0	0	0

Horseracebase ratings for the race are close for each runner. Yet **A Daay In Devon** won her race fairly comfortably. I believed she is capable of a better rating and a better speed rating. However, I did not invest this time as I was unsure about Betties Boy plus Roger Varians run of form. A Daay In Devon won at 9/2.

Al Hujaija 2nd 5/2, Beatties Boy 5th 9/4 Favourite. Better to miss a winner than back a loser though.

You can see from the previous example that following Ratings, Form Figures, or Speed Figures blindly without digging deeper does not pay. There is always more to the background of each runner.

Previously we looked at trainers in form now let us look at trainers whose horses are not in form as this is an interesting picture.

On the same day as the previous example Michael Stoute had the Favourite for the Group 3 Strensall Stakes Michaels current figures are on the following page.

Trainers

Michael Stoute

Days	Runners	Wins	Win P/L	Win%	Place	Place%
7	6	0	-6	0%	0	0%
14	8	0	-8	0%	1	13%
30	23	0	-23	0%	4	17%
60	47	8	-22.84	17%	17	36%
90	82	11	-31.01	13%	30	37%
180	134	22	-44.23	16%	59	44%
365	222	32	-86.24	14%	85	38%

Michael Has had no winners in the last 30 days and only 17% have placed. This is highly unusual for a top-class trainer such as Michael Stout. I checked his horses for the year that have started between 6/4 and 9/2 which is the range I would normally check for non-handicappers. Michael has had 21 runners in that range only two have won 9.52%. Fifteen of those started Favourite of which only one won. This is a classic case of the bookies not willing to take a chance on his horses because of his reputation. His horse in the Strensall Stakes Nostrum, started at 5/6 Favourite with Ryan Moore in the saddle. He finished last of the six runners. The race was won by the horse rated second best by HRB at 6/1.

Just for completeness Michael did have a winner and a second on the day at Windsor may be there is return to form for him around the corner. There may be value in some of his runners coming up. Also, R M Beckett who we spoke about earlier had another three winners again today too.

It pays to check trainers recent form, in the case of Michael Stout there would be good value in looking for something in the race capable of beating his runner, in the case of trainers like R M Beckett if their runners have other positives then there could be value there too.

Trainers

James Ferguson's horses have not been running well lately as can be seen from the table below.

Recent Form By Days (All Races)

	Days	Runners	Wins	Win P/L	Win%	Place	Place%
James Ferguson	7	5	0	-5	0%	2	40%
	14	24	2	-16.4	8%	7	29%
	30	45	3	-25.4	7%	12	27%
	60	78	5	-44.4	6%	21	27%
	90	111	7	-62.4	6%	31	28%
	180	169	21	-56.2	12%	57	34%
	365	245	32	-81.25	13%	87	36%

However, his horse Deauville Legend started 15/8 favourite for a £25K Listed race at Windsor eventually finishing 4th. His ratings and speed figures were also poor. The race was won by Candleford at 9/2 trained by W J Haggas whose horses are running at a 25%-win rate currently.

One of my favourite racecourses to go to and make selections from the Pre-Parade ring is Beverley. There is a meeting at Beverley today as I am writing this book. Unfortunately, I am not there today however I have a particular interest in evaluating the form of the 4:35 race. Mainly because I noticed last night that Darryl Holland's horse **Pearl Eye** is currently the forecast favourite. I have plenty of respect for Darryll both as a jockey and as a trainer I believe in the training ranks he will eventually go a long way. Currently his charges are not performing as well as expected the table of his current form is shown on the following page.

If I do my check of horses starting between 6/4 - 9/2 Darryll's horses show a profit both at SP and on the exchanges which is no surprise to me. Of the trainers in the race today only Nigel Tinklers and Michael Herringtons horses are performing better than their yearly average. This race seems too close to call so I will be watching it with interest for the future.

Trainers

Darryll Holland

Days	Runners	Wins	Win P/L	Win%	Place	Place%
7	6	0	-6	0%	0	0%
14	16	1	-13	6%	2	13%
30	28	1	-25	4%	4	14%
60	54	6	-19.4	11%	14	26%
90	79	10	-30.65	13%	20	25%
180	119	15	-16.4	13%	31	26%
365	203	22	-46.98	11%	57	28%

Result: Darryll Holland won the race with Pearl Eye 100/30 by a short head the interesting one was Michael Herrington's horse third placed Soames Forsyte 33/1 he led the race and only gave way in the closing stages that takes some doing at Beverley. On an easier course he could come up trumps next time.

Trainers

Trainer Myths

Over the many years of attending racecourses in Britain I have had many conversations with fellow enthusiasts. The one common myth that always confuses me is that it pays to follow certain trainers first time out runners. As I have mentioned before top trainer's runners including first time out are far shorter than they should be. It often pays to find a horse with experience. For example, trainers like Michael Stout or Richard Hannon Jnr. Yes, they are brilliant trainers with top class horses in their care. Michael Stout's newcomers only win on average 11% of the time compared to his annual average of 23% winners. If you check the statistics on HRB you will find that Michael Stout once had a run of 46 newcomers without a winner and in the last 10 years has only ever had 2 consecutive winning debutants once. In that time 23 of his newcomers started favourite but only four of those won. That is not a problem with Michael Stout and his training methods. That is purely the fact that bookmakers do not want to take a chance with his horses. It also lures favourite backers into backing false favourites.

Richard Hannon Jnr is another top trainer who's horses it does not pay to follow first time out. Over the last ten years less than 10% of his debutant's have won. This is close to his yearly average of 12% winners. In the last ten years only 3 years showed a slight profit at starting price. The other 7 years showed a considerable loss. Richard Hannon Jnr tends to work the opposite way to the majority of trainers. He enters his debutants in a higher class race then slowly brings them down to find their winning level. Many trainers' tend to work the other way around they give their charges an introduction in the lower classes and move them up a class as they develop.

Trainers

He once went a run of 54 consecutive losing debutants. Richard has in the last 5 years started only 10 debutants in a class 6 race. only one of the 10 won, 4 of the 10 started favourite of which none of them actually won.

You can find this pattern over and over with many of the top trainers'. It pays to do your homework if many of these trainers' horses are starting at false prices that leaves an opportunity for us to find Value for money bets elsewhere in the field.

John Gosden is probably the most successful of the top league of trainers. John Gosden's newcomers on average win 15% of the time compared to his annual average of all his runners to winners which is around 25% winners. These are massive percentage differences. The picture is slightly different for John Gosden's favourites 33% of his horses that started favourite won. It still did not pay to follow his debutants that were first or second in the market. It would have paid to follow any that were not the first two in the market 5 of the last ten years showed a profit. Of those runners that were not in the first two in the market, any that were entered in a class one or class two race only 9% won. The remainder still went a run of 31 consecutive losers but showed a profit in 5 out of the last ten years. The table below sets this out to make it clearer as I understand that it is a lot of information and numbers.

Breakdown of previous information about John Gosden

Average Winners to Runners	2&3yo 1st time out	Winning 2&3yo Favourites
25%	15%	33%

Though these are impressive figures they all show an overall loss as Johns horses are popular among the betting public. That also gives the astute punter an edge. If a top trainer's horses are going off at false prices, then there is value elsewhere in the race.

Trainers

I spend much of my time looking for horses that are either false favourites or wrongly priced by who they are trained by. There are hundreds of pieces of data that we can break John's runners down with. I will leave that to you to find out. When you break down data on the top trainers it is surprising what you can come up with. Just a word of warning here statistics tell us what has happened in the past. They are only an aid to what may happen in the future you cannot follow past statistics blindly. For example, I used to follow John Gosden's debutants closely particularly his fillies. They always ran a decent race first time out without winning then improved considerably second time out. It was as if he found their level first time out and new exactly where to place them for their following run. That could also be in a higher-class race. This year 2023 that approach seems to have changed considerably. It will be interesting to see what happens when Thady takes over the reins completely at Clarehaven.

Possibly the most successful trainer over the last four years for debutant's has been Tom Clover with 44 starts and 11 winners, 25% showing a profit at SP each of the last four years. Tom trains in Newmarket I believe he is very under rated trainer therefore his runners go off at very good value for money prices.

You can easily break any trainers' statistics down using HRB to find how they treat either their debutant's or all of their charges. It is a very useful exercise to do.

Some recent examples are A M Balding who has a record of scoring only 7% of the time, he once went a run of 64 debutants without a win. He had the favourite at Newbury on the 6th of July 2023 Clove Hitch went off the 5/6 favourite. She finished 5th beaten by the second favourite Miss Show Off who had already run two decent races at Sandown and Nottingham. Clove Hitch was beaten by over 13 lengths the second horse who also had two decent races under her belt started at 20/1.

Trainers

Ed Walker is a trainer that I am a great admirer of. In the last 4 years of his 113 debutants only 4 have won. The most recent debutant was Ten Bob Tony on the 16th of August 2023 he went off the 7/2 JF at Salisbury he finished 4th to another more experienced horse.

Another point that you may want to study about trainers is that if the Betfair SP is close to the Official SP then the horses tend to do better for some completely inexplicable reason? if the Betfair SP is considerably greater than the SP then they tend not to do so well. Not in every case of course it is like everything else to do with the sport. You need to do your homework.

You can read more about false favourites in the favourites section of this book.

It is worth checking many trainers in depth for example smaller trainers that many punters would know little about. If I picked on just one example say JR Boyle a smallish trainer that trains in Epsom. The majority of his runners are in the south he does not get the quality of horse that the top trainers get. Therefore, with the cost of travel around the country these days he limits his runners to more local areas which gives his owners better value for his charges. If he travels distances greater than 140 miles, he has a 38% strike rate showing a profit at SP every year over the last four years. Though only a slight profit in 2021 a profit none the less. Out of 217 debutants to date only one has won less than 0.5%. In the main they start at extremely long odds 100/1 plus. Yet his record for bringing horses back to the course within 7 days stands at 16% winners. Over the last ten years his runners in a class one, two or three races have shown a loss with a win of less than 7%. In classes Four, Five and Six races they have shown an overall profit on the exchanges and at SP with a win percentage of around 14% if the horse returns to the course between 16 and 60 days.

Trainers

An interesting point for traders is that in the main his runners tend to drift in the market considerably. If there is stable confidence in the horse the price tends to reduce. This of course is not always the case, but it is a particularly good guide. I have a lot of time for trainers like Jim Boyle they operate on a shoestring in comparison to the bigger trainers yet their dedication to the sport really deserves a positive mention.

There are in the UK and Ireland hundreds of trainers like Jim Boyle spending time to study them in depth is an exercise well worth doing.

Getting the feel of how trainer's horses are performing in general is a very worthwhile exercise. One thing that I do on a regular basis which only takes about five minutes is run through all the winners on a given day. Click on the trainer's profile and in the majority of cases you will find the winners are coming from stables that are in form. You will also spot horses that are beginning to perform well from yards that have had a slight lull in performances. You need to try things that others are not just to give you and edge.

The good thing about keeping notes on trainers is that you are looking for how trainer's produce their horses. Whether they start them off in a higher class then drop them when they have gained some fitness or do they go the other way around. Some trainers when they know their charges are ready to run a big race like to use the aid of a decent apprentice allowance. It is worth watching apprentice races and taking note of promising apprentices particularly if they still have a 7lb or 5lb allowance.

You can get a feel for when they are likely to do well and when their charges are not quite performing as well as expected.

I have said previously that horses are not machines and that you are expecting too much if you think they will perform the same every time they run. Keeping horses fit and finding races for them that they can win is an art.

Trainers

The following page lists trainers who have managed to get horses to win at least three times in a row. The data is taken over a ten-year period in classes 3,4,5 and 6 races. You tend to get better prices for horses that have already won twice and now they are going for a third win in a row then a fourth and so on. Most of the time handicappers do not string three or more winning races together. There is a very good reason for getting a better price third or fourth time out too. After two wins the handicapper will move the horse up in the official rating significantly. To counteract the rise in the official rating the trainer's need to move their charges up in class to lessen the burden on their backs, therefore they move up in class with a higher official rating but carry less weight. horses moving up in class may or may not be a risky betting proposition. therefore, they often start at favourable prices. A thorough check of how and why they won their previous race, then the form of their current race can be very lucrative. this works best when their previous form is from handicap races and not from Maiden or Novice races. A few trainers are excellent at this others not so. However, horses winning two non handicaps then moving to handicap company actually win 25% of the time, showing a profit at SP. The win percentage can also be improved upon with a little more form study. There was a 40/1 winner in the figures which throws the P/L out a bit.

The trainers that have pulled it off in their third race where their horses have made a profit at SP on the flat are listed in the table on the following page with the highest profit first. There are few more trainers than I have printed in the table the ones shown are the top profit-making trainers. You will be surprised if you looked at the other end of the table for trainers that have never managed to pull it off after many attempts. They too are worth making a note of as there may be value in races where they are trying to get a successive winner for the third time. The statistics are for both the UK and Ireland over a ten-year period.

Trainers

The table below shows Trainers that have managed to get horses to win three time in row and show a profit at SP.

Criteria	Win%	P/L(SP)	P/L(BF)
Thompson, D W	100	28	38.95
Mulvany, Michael	50	26.33	32.13
Main, Mrs H S	50	25	29.05
Moore, G L	27.59	22.43	32.33
Ward, Tom	50	20.5	24.07
Hollinshead, Steph	50	19.25	23.7
Cox, C G	26.09	18.68	28.52
Frost, Kevin	37.5	15.25	23.87
Slattery, Andrew	40	13.75	15.75
Dwyer, C A	40	13	13.9
Chamings, P R	40	12.63	14.28
Tinkler, N	31.25	12	20.8
Ryan, K A	24.32	12	15.01
Kirby, P A	31.58	11.83	14.82
Carroll, D	26.09	11.67	15.13
Dalgleish, Keith	25.49	10.18	13.52
Bravery, G C	50	10	13.25
George, Paul	100	10	14.93
Halford, M	33.33	9.33	10.82
Ryan, J	60	9.25	9.98
Dixon, Scott	26.67	9.2	14.28
Nicholls, Adrian	50	9.08	10.28
McBride, P J	41.67	9	10.6
Bridger, J / Cook, R	28.57	8.76	12.6
Lupini, Miss Natalia	60	8.5	10.23

Trainers

There are certain trainers whose runners get supported in the market during the day or quite late on these are not all successful. Following horses that are supported in the market from opening as the third or fourth favourite then getting backed into favouritism would result in a substantial loss overall. If you follow the trainers whose runners do get backed in from third or fourth favourite to favouritism and do make a profit the exercise is very worthwhile to keep a list of such trainers. The following page shows a table of the trainers who have made a profit at SP over the last 10 years when their horses have been supported into favouritism. These trainers have made a profit every year in the last 10 years.

If you looked at the other end of the table, you would find the usual trainers that we have mentioned before. Top trainers that have many horses in their care. You may think that there must be away to make a profit from these trainers. The problem is trainers like Aiden O'Brien have so many top-class horses in their care. Bookmakers never take a chance with his horses the prices are so restrictive. He would need to have such a high strike rate to get him anywhere near halfway up the table. The only way that I found to make these trainers pay is to individually study each trainer's methods. Keep notes and keep rechecking on the strengths of the stable.

On pages 83 and 85 I have printed two tables page 85 are trainers whose horses have drifted in the market and made a profit at SP. On page 84 are trainers whose horses have shortened in the market and made a loss. The tables are top and bottom in each case with a host of trainers in between. None of the information in the trainers' tables cast any sort assertion on the trainers'. It is not down to the trainers whether their charges drift or shorten in the market. The interesting thing is Aiden O'Brien is the top of the table for horses that drift in the market but still win and make a nice profit.

Trainers

How much of this shortening and drifting in the market is now down to Traders where the interest in Trading is gathering pace I would not know.

The facts over ten years speak for themselves you can spot similar things with all trainers. There will be some sort of pattern in areas where they excel and areas where they fall short. Nothing will work out 100% of the time but the more work and interest you put into looking for angles the luckier you will become.

Trainers

Trainers whose horses have shown a profit every year over the last 10 years when backed into favouritism from third or fourth favourite in the opening market, Flat and All Weather

Criteria	Bets	Wins	Win%	P/L(SP)
Burke, K R	203	72	35.47	66.19
Tinkler, N	81	29	35.8	34.63
Beckett, R M	258	90	34.88	28.66
Varian, Roger	204	71	34.8	27.48
Carr, Mrs R A	104	29	27.88	27
Shaw, D	37	16	43.24	26.54
Walker, Ed	166	54	32.53	25.55
Haggas, W J	216	74	34.26	25.28
Wall, C F	76	27	35.53	23.85
Harrington, Mrs John	113	36	31.86	23.22
Johnston, M	376	119	31.65	23.21
Williams, S C	159	54	33.96	23.11
Scott, George	35	14	40	20.7
Fell, R / Murray, S	95	31	32.63	20.32
Perratt, Miss L A	22	11	50	17.01
Brittain, Antony	41	13	31.71	16.83
Dwyer, C A	41	17	41.46	16.56
Moore, J S	16	7	43.75	14.75
Tuite, Joseph	42	16	38.1	14.21
Oshea, J G M	16	7	43.75	13.75
Menuisier, David	30	11	36.67	13.75
Gollings, S	7	4	57.14	12.75

Trainers

This is the other end of the table. These results are still from horses opening in the market as 3rd or 4th favourite and get backed into favouritism. This table shows trainers who made the least profit.

Criteria	Bets	Wins	Win%	P/L(SP)
Ellison, B	97	21	21.65	-18.97
Herrington,M	38	5	13.16	-19.29
Tregoning, M P	40	6	15	-19.75
Cox, C G	145	39	26.9	-19.83
OBrien, A P	170	51	30	-20.16
Ryan, J	44	7	15.91	-21.37
King, A	64	13	20.31	-21.49
Palmer, Hugo	110	27	24.55	-21.56
McConnell, John C	34	3	8.82	-23.62
Appleby, Charlie	144	39	27.08	-23.67
Prescott, Sir Mark	63	13	20.63	-23.85
Suroor, Saeed Bin	160	45	28.13	-24.93
Quinn, J J	126	26	20.63	-25.01
Dascombe, Tom	121	28	23.14	-25.61
Dixon, Scott	55	7	12.73	-26
McCreery, W	68	10	14.71	-28.24
Evans, P D	170	39	22.94	-30.63
Botti, M	121	26	21.49	-37.98
Ryan, K A	170	40	23.53	-41.16
Loughnane, Daniel Mark	72	7	9.72	-45.75
Hughes, Richard	125	24	19.2	-49.7
Easterby, T D	296	66	22.3	-52.76
Hannon (Jnr), Richard	280	59	21.07	-69.18

Trainers

This table shows trainer's who have the highest return at SP when their horses drift from favouritism to 3rd or 4th in the market.

Criteria	Bets	Wins	Win%	P/L(SP)
OBrien, A P	134	32	23.88	45.33
Williams, Ian	46	14	30.43	40
Wigham, M	26	10	38.46	35.5
Carroll, A W	118	23	19.49	33.75
Hammond, Micky	21	6	28.57	19.5
Nicholls, D	16	6	37.5	19.5
Goldie, J S	42	9	21.43	19
King, A	29	8	27.59	18.83
Wilson, N	6	4	66.67	18.83
Simcock, D M	75	16	21.33	18.5
Frost, Kevin	14	4	28.57	17.5
McBride, P J	16	5	31.25	17
Macey, Jessica	10	4	40	16.5
Mulvany, Michael	13	4	30.77	15
Midgley, P T	51	10	19.61	14.75
Boughey, George	65	13	20	14.49
Fellowes, Charlie	29	7	24.14	14
Loughnane, David	31	8	25.81	13.5
Foy, Kevin	24	5	20.83	13.5
Morrison, H	37	6	16.22	12.83
Levins, J F	29	6	20.69	12.5
Tompkins, M H	8	3	37.5	11
Phelan, P M	4	2	50	11
Clover, Tom	17	4	23.53	11

Trainers

This table shows trainer's who have the lowest return at SP when their horses drift from favouritism to 3rd or 4th in the market.

Criteria	Bets	Wins	Win%	P/L(SP)
Jenkins, J R	21	0	0	-21
Appleby, M	140	20	14.29	-21.5
Weld, D K	106	14	13.21	-21.67
Cowell, R M H	72	9	12.5	-22
Moore, G L	44	5	11.36	-22.25
Stoute, Sir Michael	106	15	14.15	-22.5
Slattery, Andrew	28	1	3.57	-22.5
Williams, S C	83	10	12.05	-23
Evans, P D	71	8	11.27	-24
Dunlop, E A L	73	9	12.33	-24.67
Bolger, J S	67	7	10.45	-26.5
Fahey, R A	194	28	14.43	-27.5
Beckett, R M	62	6	9.68	-28.17
Dods, M	78	8	10.26	-30.5
Burke, K R	75	8	10.67	-31
Halford, M	45	2	4.44	-31
Quinn, J J	91	11	12.09	-32.25
Easterby, T D	130	17	13.08	-34.75
Ellison, B	46	2	4.35	-35
Gosden, J H M	186	26	13.98	-35.42
OBrien, Joseph Patrick	100	9	9	-41.75
Hannon (Jnr), Richard	205	28	13.66	-43
Johnston, M	228	32	14.04	-52.84
OMeara, D	207	22	10.63	-78.84

Trainers

Your ability to manipulate data to find patterns is endless. Let us for example look at trainers who bring their new recruits out for their first racecourse appearance and win first time out.

You can select all runners having their first outing and in non-handicaps then list all trainers sort them either by Wins, Win% or Profit/Loss at SP. even by Place% if that is what floats your boat. Pick on one trainer then break those results down even further to see if you can find a pattern.

Let us take G.M Lyons for example if you break down his debutants. You will find that if he brings them out in a class 3-4 race, they are more successful than in a class 5 or 6 race *(Ireland do not have races broken down to classes as they do in the UK, HRB does have a tab where you can classify them into classes)* this tells me that he knows when he has a horse with ability. If they fail to win first time out, they often win before their fourth racecourse appearance. Also, the results are less consistent when the going is either Heavy or softer than Good to Soft. This is the case with any form you can analyse that in itself is another great sauce of winners if you sort the data properly.

If their first race is over 6 Furlongs, he has a win rate greater than 31%. If he travels the 215 miles to Killarney, he is 3 from 3, 40% at Cork too. As I keep saying the possibilities are endless you just need to specialise. Find a niche and run with it. Do not get disappointed and keep jumping from one thing to another. I also have to say everything is based on historical data. It is not a guarantee of what will happen in the future, but it is a very good guide. Break the data down as much as you like the more data you have the more dependable it is. For example, 300 from 1000 sets of data is better than 3 from 10 and so on. It may pay to follow certain trainer's patterns rather than relying on racecourse form. Due to the better prices you will get looking at an angle that nobody else is.

Class

Class

When talking about class people have differing views, that is ok, we all need to follow what we believe. Some talk about the class of a race, others talk about the class of a particular horse.

I will give you an extreme example, I was talking to a fellow enthusiast only a few weeks ago. Putting the world to rights about differing situations within racing. We got onto the subject of class. I for a very long time thought we were on the same page when it comes to evaluating the class of a horse. However, I was wrong, Stupidly I mentioned Frankel as being the classiest horse we will ever see in a very long time. He came back with *"How do you know that"* I went on to reel off Frankel's races who he beat the distance he beat them by etc. He came back with *"He didn't win a handicap though did he"* I was shocked at his reply, so I replied sarcastically *"I am not sure if you are aware, but Handicap's and Group races are not quite the same thing. Horses at the top range of handicap races may move successfully or not into Listed and Group company"* to which he replied *"He never carried two stone more than the rest of the field and won convincingly did he"* I am now thinking we have been in here too long and he must have been drinking before we got here. Again, I replied, *"we are talking about Frankel not Arkel"* Too cut a very long story short. His interpretation of a classy horse is one that firstly wins then the handicapper keeps upping the official rating and it doesn't matter what the handicapper does he cannot stop the horse winning even at the top level. I did point out that would depend on the confirmation of the horse and his weight carrying capacity and that a jockey may be able to run faster than a weightlifter but if you kept lumping stones on top of each, there would come a point that the weight lifter would win the race and the jockey would collapse under the burden. To which he replied *"Exactly, so Frankel never had that weight lumped on him, so we do not truly know if he was the best ever"* at which point I decided it was time to change the conversation.

Class

The preceding page shows that people can have completely differing views about the class of a horse.

I do not intend to get into that sort of differing views again. To be clear, what I am talking about here is the class of a race and the horses in it. A class 6 race does not always mean the horses in the race could never win a class 4 for example. Alternatively, horses racing in a class 4 race does not mean they will waltz away with a class 6 race despite the weight they may carry.

17th Jul 2023 - Ayr 15:45:00

Ayr Gold Cup Trial Handicap

Distance: **6f (1320 yards)** Prize (winner): **£15462** Dir: **Straight**

Runners: **16** Going: **Good to Soft** Class: **Class 3** Age Restrictions: **3yo+**

The above race is the Ayr Gold cup trial which is the fore runner to the Ayr Gold cup. The trial is always hotly contested. I just cannot understand why punters made Thunder Roar the 7/2 favourite. It is absolutely bazar. It could be that punters were drawn in by the favourite and had Thunder Roar in multiple bets. Or that the bookies had large liabilities over the favourite of the race. Therefore, made sure Thunder Roar was the very risky favourite. Whatever it was Thunder Roar did not deserve favouritism. He was a false favourite, and you will see mentions of false favourites, and how to profit from them throughout this book.

Thunder Roar had won a class 5 £4K race 7 days previously. The race was not hotly contested it was a typical class 5 race. He had never been tried over 6 furlongs his first race as a 2yo was over 7 furlongs. That tells me that his trainer at that time thought he was a stayer rather than a sprinter. His breeding would bear that out. the Ayr race that he won was a Monday race you will read about the importance of that several times in this book.

There were others in the race with far better credentials.

Class

Like Music Society who had been running in Class 2 £38K races and finishing close up trained by Tim Easterby who targets these sort of races. I admit trying to predict when Tim Easterby's horses are going to win is like trying to catch fog, he is still a trainer I admire and fear in certain races.

Illusionist had been running in High value class 2 and class 3 races all his career he only ran in a class 4 race twice winning one and 2nd in the other early on in his career. Music Society was 2nd at 11/1 Illusionist was 4th at 16/1, I could make a case for most of these except Thunder Roar. He has since run again in a class 4 £10K race and once again was soundly beaten finishing 13/17 beaten by 18 Lengths. Thunder Roar will have his day maybe he needs to drop in official ratings and get back to a class 5 race before progressing slowly.

The story of Thunder Roar happens every day in handicaps up and down the country.

Male V Female

I just want to mention the difference in the sexes when it comes to class and performance. The table on the following page shows the performance of Males verses Female over the last 5 years that won last time out then reappeared in a higher class and higher prize money. Again, the numbers are taken from Horseracebase and are readily available for all to see and check. Females win more than 2% fewer times than Males. With half the races in the assessment they have lost just as much money at SP on Betfair the Males have shown a profit. Though I would not get too carried away with that as I did notice one horse that won at 28/1 paid 65/1 on Betfair and there may be others that did the same there is a table on the following page.

Class

Criteria	Bets	Wins	Win%	P/L(SP)	P/L(BF)
Male	5993	980	16.35	-724.52	86.21
Female	2774	393	14.17	-705.53	-462.58

The situation for Mares verses Fillies is very much the same. Fillies win 2% more often than Mares *(A Female horse older than four years old)* when moved up in class and prize money. The situation is the same whether on the Flat or on the All Weather.

Now let us look at the differences in the two sexes when carrying a higher weight than their winning weight.

Criteria	Bets	Wins	Win%	P/L(SP)	P/L(BF)
Male	3906	992	25.4	-249.69	105.33
Female	1575	323	20.51	-311.65	-174.77

Males carrying a higher weight than their last time out winning weight win again 25.4% of the time over the last 5 years. Females win again 20.51% of the time a difference of very nearly 5%. Again, the males show a profit on the exchanges.

A more interesting statistic is shown below taken over 8 years.

Criteria	Bets	Wins	Win%	P/L(SP)	P/L(BF)
Colt	1111	374	33.66	-41.55	60.96
Horse	61	21	34.43	5.66	9.06
Gelding	4925	1101	22.36	-593.74	-126.13
Filly	2053	439	21.38	-390.5	-214.62
Mare	435	84	19.31	-57.74	-17.3

Class

In the last eight years Colts and Horses that won their last race then carried more weight next time out. Win more than 10% more often than geldings. Again, Fillies win 2% more often than Mares under the same criteria.

Under certain conditions Fillies and Mares on the All-Weather when starting favourite are extremely unreliable. Compared to the same conditions on the flat. I set up a system back in 2020 to pick out Females on the All Weather that were the forecast favourite when there are more than 30% of males in the race. They win on average only 17% of the time. As I have mentioned before I do not lay horses, nor do I trade. I use this system to see if I can find a Male in the race to beat the forecast favourite. There was just such a race today at Wolverhampton. I cannot for the life of me work out why punters or the bookmakers thought Beenham was a worthy favourite in this race. This is a five-horse race there are two Fillies Beenham and Make it Easy. Two Colts Hint Of the Jungle and Law Of Average and one Gelding Lieutenant Rascal (IRE). I have copied below My adjusted ratings to bring all their past performances to 100% taken from HRB Standard ratings then the speed ratings.

HRB Ratings levelled to 100% for the last two races

Horse	C/G/F	Odds	LR	2LR
Hint Of The Jungle (IRE)	Colt	7/2	91.4	77.9
Beenham (IRE)	Filly	2/1	79.4	95.5
Lieutenant Rascal (IRE)	Gelding	5/2	91.1	77.2
Make It Easy (IRE)	Filly	3/1	62.4	58.7
Law Of Average	Colt	80/1	47.6	0

Class
HRB Speed Ratings

Horse	C/G/F	Odds	LR	2LR
Hint Of The Jungle (IRE)	Colt	7/2	72.04	69.32
Beenham (IRE)	Filly	2/1	66.68	84.64
Lieutenant Rascal (IRE)	Gelding	5/2	66.64	64.92
Make It Easy (IRE)	Filly	3/1	70.84	60.4
Law Of Average	Colt	80/1	56.09	0

You can see from these two tables firstly Hint Of The Jungle's Last race was far superior to Beenham's last race. Lieutenant Rascal had a very similar rating to Beenham. Beenham's 2LR was quite good however she did not reproduce that next time out. Again, Hint of The Jungle and Lieutenant Rascal 2LR were similar. Plus, the fact they both showed improvement.

From the HRB Speed ratings you can see that both Hint Of The Jungle and Lieutenant Rascal both showed improved form from their respective 2LR. Beenham did not do that. Plus, the fact that we previously established that Colts perform on average better than Geldings and Geldings perform on average better than fillies the result was.

1st Hint Of the Jungle 7/2
2nd Lieutenant Rascal 5/2
3rd Make It Easy 3/1
4th Beenham 2/1Fav
5th Law of Average 80/1

Beenham was a false favourite. I found this race by looking for Fillies on the All Weather that were forecast favourites. It did not take much working out which horse to have an interest in. The ratings showed that it would be close between the first two and so it was there was just a Neck separating them at the post with the Colt getting the better of the Gelding.

Class

It does not always work out as simple as that. In the last race on the card a 2nd favourite Filly easily beat the favourite Gelding. The gelding had better ratings but poor speed ratings where as the Filly had very good speed ratings. That was a race to leave alone though.

On the following page I have reprinted a screen from HRB that they provide to instantly show you horses that are either up or down in class from their previous race. Whether the track is the same, distance +/-, weight +/- and days since the horse last ran. It is an extremely valuable table that gets produced for every race and can save you so much time looking for the information. I apologise for the sideways printing but unfortunately it was necessary to fit it onto the page.

Horses that are dropped in class are clearly worth looking at in terms of an investment opportunity in a race. However, a drop in class does not mean they are going to be superior in the race to any other. Data bares that out if a horse has been dropped even by four classes. If it was beaten by 5-10+ lengths. Most of the time he would have been racing out of his class. We have spoken earlier about trainers that can exploit a drop-in class. That is another thing altogether you are far better looking for actual form. Horses improving or running well in the class they are currently entered in. this can be demonstrated by the table printed on page 97

RACE	HORSE	TRACK	CLASS (1-7)	DISTANCE	TRAINER	JOCKEY	WEIGHT	RACE TYPE	DAYS
2.00 Pontefract	Curran (IRE)		+1	SAME		SAME	+6 lbs	SAME (Novices)	20
2.00 Pontefract	Prepschool (IRE)		-2	+2f			+2 lbs	SAME (Novices)	51
2.00 Pontefract	Cestrian Spirit (IRE)		SAME	+2.5f			-3 lbs	SAME (Novices)	18
2.00 Pontefract	Love Safari (IRE)		SAME	+2f		SAME	SAME	SAME (Novices)	32
2.00 Pontefract	Synchronize (IRE)		SAME	+2f			+2 lbs	Novices / Maiden	11
2.00 Pontefract	The Hun (IRE)		+1	SAME		SAME	SAME	SAME (Novices)	20
2.00 Pontefract	Flavor		-2	+3f			-3 lbs	Novices / Maiden	24
2.30 Pontefract	Invincible Molly		SAME	SAME		SAME	+7 lbs	Hcp Nursery / Novices	16
2.30 Pontefract	Count Palatine (IRE)		IRE	-1f			+4 lbs	Hcp Nursery / Non-Hcp	16
2.30 Pontefract	Validated		+1	-1.5f			+1 lbs	Hcp Nursery / Maiden	25
2.30 Pontefract	Catton Lady	SAME	+1	SAME		SAME	+4 lbs	Hcp Nursery / Novices	18
2.30 Pontefract	Havana Rose (IRE)		+1	+1f		SAME	-1 lbs	Hcp Nursery / Novices	20
2.30 Pontefract	Beechwood Star (IRE)		IRE	SAME			+1 lbs	Hcp Nursery / Non-Hcp	25
2.30 Pontefract	Willolarupi (IRE)		+1	+1f		SAME	+1 lbs	Hcp Nursery / Maiden	19
2.30 Pontefract	Chumbaa (IRE)		SAME	+1f		SAME	+6 lbs	SAME (Hcp Nursery)	14
2.30 Pontefract	Salamanca Lad (IRE)		+2	SAME			-6 lbs	SAME (Hcp Nursery)	21
2.30 Pontefract	Inspiring Speeches (IRE)		SAME	-1.5f			-7 lbs	Hcp Nursery / Novices	18
2.30 Pontefract	Oceanic Wonder		+1	-1f			-7 lbs	SAME (Hcp Nursery)	16
3.00 Pontefract	Metahorse		SAME	+0.5f		SAME	+2 lbs	SAME (Handicap)	13
3.00 Pontefract	Indiana Be	SAME	SAME	SAME		SAME	-1 lbs	SAME (Handicap)	18
3.00 Pontefract	In These Shoes (IRE)		-1	-1f		SAME	+9 lbs	SAME (Handicap)	10
3.00 Pontefract	Eastern Charm (IRE)		SAME	SAME		SAME	-1 lbs	SAME (Handicap)	19
3.00 Pontefract	Tobetso (IRE)		+1	SAME		SAME	-6 lbs	SAME (Handicap)	18
3.00 Pontefract	Create (IRE)		+1	+1f			-4 lbs	Handicap / Novices	33
3.00 Pontefract	My Honey B		+2	SAME		SAME	-15 lbs	SAME (Handicap)	38
3.00 Pontefract	Mount King (IRE)	SAME	SAME	SAME			-1 lbs	SAME (Handicap)	18
3.00 Pontefract	Tasever		+1	+1f		SAME	-8 lbs	SAME (Handicap)	26

Class

The list below shows class changes over a ten-year period. It goes from upped in class by 8 classes to dropped in class by 8 classes obviously the percentages get better and better. The list is for all horses that were either moved up or down in class,

Criteria	Bets	Wins	Win%	P/L(SP)
Drop 8	6	2	33.33	-0.84
Drop 7	53	19	35.85	22.76
Drop 6	157	49	31.21	-29.88
Drop 5	353	82	23.23	-67.4
Drop 4	1298	238	18.34	-211.95
Drop 3	4553	747	16.41	-813.62
Drop 2	19014	2422	12.74	-3965.21
Drop 1	99591	11460	11.51	-22692.25
Same	281491	31220	11.09	-62928.35
Up 1	83707	9050	10.81	-21022.61
Up 2	16685	1824	10.93	-3598.9
Up 3	5348	495	9.26	-1901.67
Up 4	2072	181	8.74	-605.15
Up 5	802	59	7.36	-269.51
Up 6	385	23	5.97	-6.66
Up 7	48	1	2.08	-45
Up 8	3	0	0	-3

Class

If we change the data to horses that were beaten by 3 lengths or less last time out and were either moved up or down in class. You may expect an improvement in those dropped in class. There is a slight improvement, but it is negligible and still they do not make a profit at SP overall. I am not saying ignore movements in class either up or down, do your homework on the trainer to see if it is a move, he/she makes on a regular basis. Or they may be dropping a horse in class if that is aligned with traveling further than they would normally do. If I have an interest in a horse dropped in class, there needs to be another reason for supporting it.

Criteria	Bets	Wins	Win%	P/L(SP)
Drop 8	1	1	100	2.25
Drop 7	3	1	33.33	-1.67
Drop 6	6	2	33.33	-2.55
Drop 5	21	7	33.33	-10.35
Drop 4	110	35	31.82	-11.73
Drop 3	586	205	34.98	33.1
Drop 2	3072	699	22.75	-429.7
Drop 1	22745	4308	18.94	-3615.64
Same	98288	16614	16.9	-16208.75
Up 1	41931	6272	14.96	-8095.07
Up 2	11034	1513	13.71	-1524.22
Up 3	4070	460	11.3	-1096.02
Up 4	1829	171	9.35	-505.1
Up 5	746	57	7.64	-247.51
Up 6	350	22	6.29	-122.66
Up 7	42	1	2.38	-39
Up 8	2	0	0	-2

Speed Figures

Speed Figures

Once again going back to the days of the Sporting Life they used to produce speed figures in their form guide pages. At the time I found these very useful in certain circumstances. If I remember correctly, I found them most useful for horses changing codes from Flat racing to National Hunt racing.

I am not sure when Horseracebase started producing speed figures. Like everything Chris and his team do they give their customers options as to how they use them and what they want out of them. Speed Figures are a recent addition to Horseracebase and I believe they are still being refined How they compare to Timeform speed ratings I do not know but I find them perfectly good enough for my needs without making any alteration myself.

How much importance you place on Speed Figures is entirely up to you. Personally, they are not the top of my agenda when making selections. but I do use them to check back on the quality of races In which I am interested. Unfortunately, in this country split times per furlong are not as readily available as they should be though they are slowly beginning to creep in. We are some way off the degree of precision that is used in America. For us the timing is from the start of the race to the end. That does not tell you whether the first half of a race was run slowly with a sprint finish. If it did, I am not sure how much importance I would place on that if any.

I will explain why I place some importance on Speed Figures but also, they do not form a major part of my decision making. On the following page is a race run at Catterick on the 12th of September 2023. There are two flip flopping favourites between Wades Magic and Langholm if we look at the speed figures, last time out speed figures. Guest List stands out with a rating of 68.13. A she had never achieved anything like this before I thought I would check out why she has suddenly jumped to that figure last time out.

Speed Figures

Below are the speed figures for the 3:10 at Catterick on the 12th of September 2023. You can see the speed figure for Guest List's last race stands out at 68.13.

Horse	Rating	Odds	L	2L
Langholm (IRE)	64.32	3/1	61.52	67.93
Redrosezorro	63.94	7/2	63.31	31.64
Wades Magic	63.82	5/2	65.09	61.45
Guest List	62.66	9/1	68.13	57.51
Gunnerside (IRE)	62.32	17/2	58.39	35.11
Havana Rum (IRE)	59.31	9/2	67.67	55.65

She finished 7th of 13 at Southwell. She ran in a Class 6 Hcp over 6f Division 2 both divisions of that race were run exceptionally quick for 6F at Southwell on standard going, 3.03seconds and 2.89 Seconds faster than the standard time. In fact, there was a third race at Southwell a few days later also run in a very fast time. The time is quicker than the average on going classed as Standard to Fast. Also, All races on that day were ran particularly quick for Standard Going at Southwell. The race run over 1m 4f won by Fox Flame was 5.3 seconds faster than the average for the course. This to me shows that the officials had got the assessment of the going wrong. It was clearly Standard to Fast if not just Fast. Horseracebase can only go on what the officials describe the going to be. Therefore, a bit of caution needs to be added when relying purely on the speed figures.

Speed Figures

In today's race at Catterick The two joint favourites are trained by Tim Easterby (Wades Magic) and M.Dods (Langholm) both trainers have a win percentage for horses that start favourite in their care of 26%. Tim's runners to winner's ratio currently is down to 4% from his annual average of 8%. Michael Dods winners to runners currently are running at 22% compared to his annual average of 11%. Clearly the trainer whose horses are bang in form is the trainer of Langholm.

The other horse in the race with a good Speed figure last time out is Havana Rum. Though he is at the bottom of the table in the overall ratings he certainly needs checking to see why he had such a good rating. Trained by Richard Fahey whose winner to runners stands at 19% compared to annual average of 13% so no problem there. All other races on the day from Havana Rum's previous race bar the NXT Handicap over 1m3f were timed at slower than average that makes Havana Rums time correct and a substantial improvement for him. He should give the two joint favourites something to think about. I did not invest in any of the runners, but I will watch the race with a great deal of interest.

Result
1st Havana Rum 5/1
2nd Langholm 5/2 J/F
3rd Wades Magic 5/2 J
6th Guest List 11/1

It is quite satisfying knowing that you have worked the race out correctly. Slightly disappointing that you did not invest but the pleasure for me is getting the result right.

Speed Figures

Now having said all that the information on speed figures provided by Horseracebase is simply nothing short of remarkable. I used to keep my own Speed figures on a massive spreadsheet with hundreds of pages of data. I do not have to do that anymore as Chris and his team does a far better job for me. The information provided is far too much for me to reprint here. You could spend weeks and weeks sifting through the speed figure data looking for and finding angles to work with. I love working through data and maybe one day I will start to look at the race and how they were run. whether or not the speed figure provided could have been bettered or not. You can look at data for every single race compared by class for every course and every distance on every type of going. You could pick out fast run races to see if they were genuine or not. or slow run race to see if the going was reported correctly. If you like your data, then fill your boots with speed figures on Horseracebase.

Having said all that, I just need to point out why Speed Ratings are so fickle for any horse other than the winner. You can never be sure what the exact speed rating should be. let us say a horse was beaten by two lengths unless we do more homework was he catching the winner or losing ground to the winner. Did the winner win comfortably in which case our horse beaten by two lengths may not deserve the rating it did get. Did the horse that finished second have bad luck in running and get caught up in traffic or did it have free run of the race. Without watching the race, you will never know.

Speed Figures

If that is the case for a horse that was beaten by two lengths or more the further they get beaten the more the speed figure could be of little value. To demonstrate let us look at a race run on 17th September 2023. On a day when not a single top-rated horse on speed figures won. The last two races of each horse are shown in the table below.

Horse	Rating	Odds	L	2L
Rogue Force	65.89	11/2	44.71	61.89
Turbo Command	61.27	4/1	48.34	55.26
Doomsday	58.53	7/2	58.13	52.13
Kalama Sunrise	58.44	11/2	62.76	45.52
Spartakos	57.92	9/4	61.45	59.25
Indian Outlaw	55.82	14/1	55.01	59.67

On this occasion we are not looking at the overall rating of the runners, but I do like to check the figure for each of the runners' last race. We can see in this race that we have two that stand out above the rest. Kalama Sunrise and Spartakos, Kala Sunrise has the best speed rating last time out, but does she represent value at 11/2. If we check her form, we will see that she may have run in a class 2 race last time out but she was 13/13 beaten 26.7 lengths. In her penultimate race she was 7/7 beaten 24.7 lengths. There is no way that we can accurately measure those performances. Other than to say they are poor.

If we look at the form of Spartiakos he has been running in class 6 races. Last time out he was 5/13 beaten 2.9 lengths. The reason I noticed this is because I like to check out the chances of horses that finished outside the first four but were beaten by less than 3 lengths.

Speed Figures

As they could represent excellent value for money. The rating for Spartakos is far more likely to be accurate than the rating for Kalama Sunrise. there was nothing else in the race that looked likely to be close.

The result of the race was that Spartakos won at 9/4 being eased down considerably at the end. The ratings for each of their last races were near enough correct Spartakos was an absolute steel in the race. Also being eased down means his speed figure next time out will not be a true measure of his ability. Just to prove another point in situations like this Spartakos is a gelding Kalama Sunrise is a filly that was another plus for Spartakos.

In the preceding race to this we had the same situation the table is shown below.

Horse	Rating	Odds	L	2L
Graces Quest	64.87	11/2	57.21	69.49
Golden Valour	62.73	17/2	59.61	62.72
Smart Lass	62	5/2	65.93	66.48
Blue Antares	59.83	3/1	60.11	60.57
Spanish Hustle	55.44	9/4	64.54	57.8

The last race of the two market leaders are superior to the rest of the field. Spanish Hustle was fourth of eleven, beaten by 1.9L in class 5 £4K race. Smart lass was sixth of seven beaten by 8.2 Lengths in a Class 6 £3K race. Again, we have the Gelding against the Filly. How the two are close in the market is anybody's guess. Spanish Hustle won the race at 9/4 Smart Lass was last of the five runners.

Speed Figures

In the race preceding that one we have the below situation.

Horse	Rating	Odds	L	2L
Rock Melody	75.48	8/11	76.24	69.68
Water Of Leith	73.07	10/1	70.36	71.39
Princess Karine	72.64	9/4	75.52	71
Ramon Di Loria	71.51	8/1	54.87	63.12

Once again two horses clear of the rest last time out. Rock Melody is the 8/11 favourite; Princess Karine is 9/4. Rock Melody's last race was a class 2 £52K race finished 7/18 Beaten by 9.1 Lengths, Princess Karine's last race was a Class 3 £10K race Beaten by 1.8 Lengths, in this case they are both Fillies. Princess Karine's rating is far more likely to be accurate.

The result was that Princess Karine Won at 9/4 beating Rock Melody the odds-on favourite.

Three races in a row with virtually the same situations. This works out best in races with 6 runners or less where there are two that are above the rest last time out. It shows an excellent way of using speed figures to your advantage. However, you still need to do further checks, you still need to watch the races of each runner, you still need to evaluate if the ratings are correct.

Speed Figures

Now let us look at a race with more runners where it is not so obvious just by looking at the numbers.

3:05 Brighton 18th September 2023
Apprentice Handicap 1M2f.

Below is a copy of the speed ratings produced by Horseracebase. Again, HRB produce many more columns I have just reprinted the ones that for me are essential.

Horse	Rating	Odds	L	2L
Long Call	68.39	20/1	73.99	67.8
Meadram	63.33	6/1	72.38	61.62
Send In The Clouds	57.62	4/1	63.44	48.03
Bbob Alula	59.28	28/1	60.32	55.4
Florence Street	63.69	50/1	59.65	0
Tamay Girl	57.93	33/1	58.89	56.71
Billaki Mou	55.87	11/2	57.28	53.64
Platinum Prince	61.47	15/2	54.87	60.72
Miss Harmony	64.7	5/1	54.76	62.64
Habenero Star	59.98	4/1	52.79	60.7
Decisive Call (IRE)	54.6	10/1	48.33	53.42

I have sorted the table by (Last Race) you can sort all tables that HRB produce by their column headers. As you know I put considerable emphasis on the speed rating of the horse's last race. We have two horses at the head of the ratings. Long Call 20/1 and Meadram 6/1. To save describing each horse individually I have created a table of the main points.

Speed Ratings

Horse	LR	Class	Btn By	Sex	SP
Long Call	73.99	4	-19.7L	G	20/1
Meadram	72.38	5	-8.1L	G	6/1
Send In The Clouds	63.44	6	+4.8L	G	4/1
Bbob Alua	60.32	6	-6.6L	G	28/1
Florence Street	59.65	6	-13.2L	M	50/1
Tamay Girl	58.89	5	-5.6L	F	33/1
Billaki Mou	57.28	6	-8.9L	G	11/2
Miss Harmony	54.76	6	-Nk	F	5/1
Habanero Star	52.79	5	-6L	M	4/1

Going on what we discussed previously where would you want your money to be. Long Call's rating comes from a Hurdle race where he was well beaten. All the rest besides Send in the Clouds were also well Beaten. Send in the clouds Won by 4.8 Lengths it looks like the only horse to get near him is Miss Harmony a Filly. Habanero Star is Joint Favourite Beaten 6 Lengths last time and is a Mare. There really is no choice but either select Send In The Clouds or leave the race alone. Send in the Clouds won the race by 3.5 Lengths Habanero Star was third.

Let us look at another race on the same day

16:05 Thirsk

Blue Sky Event Services Selling Handicap

Distance: 6f (1320 yards) Prize (winner): £4187 Dir: Straight

Runners: 10   Going: Soft Class: Class 6   Age Restrictions: 3-6yo

The Table for this race is on the following page the race was won by Captain Dandy starting the 11/4 (Fav). Captain Dandy was top rated overall also top-rated last time out. He finished 6/12 last time out but he was only beaten 2.3 Lengths the fact that he was 6/12 to me means there could be value in his price.

Speed Ratings

I purposely look for horses like this as I have previously mentioned. The fact that he was top-rated for speed and top-rated last time out was a bonus. When I checked other horses out, there is no other horse in the race that got that close to the winner.

My point is that if Captain Dandy had finished second beaten by the same distance his price would have been much shorter which is nonsense I know. But that is the way it seems to work. Captain Dandy just had Plus written all over him and 11/4 was excellent value for money.

Horse	Rating	Odds	L	2L
Captain Dandy (IRE)	57.82	11/4	59.28	57.21
Strip Out	56.58	20/1	58.35	47.11
Kasino	58.12	28/1	57.35	53.2
Jazzagal (IRE)	57.46	6/1	56.36	52.44
Howyadoin (IRE)	59.1	13/2	56.2	68.32
Smooch (IRE)	56.1	9/2	55.99	60.08
Captain Corcoran (IRE)	58.03	12/1	54.24	59.28
Wregate Lad IRE)	56.29	12/1	53.96	56.45
Mai Award	56.33	14/1	46.28	58.98
Hot Scoop	59.87	13/2	40.93	61.56

Let us look at racing on the following day. This time we will look at a different way of using the figures that is also very effective.

Tue 19th Sep 2023
2.15 Yarmouth (7 runners)
AKS Skip Hire Services Nursery
7f (1543 yards)
Class 5, Good To Soft, 2yo, Win: £4397

Speed Ratings

Horseracebase allows you to arrange the table into any order you want. The first table is arranged by the 4th last race of each horse then the 2nd table is arranged by the 3rd last race of each horse so on to the last table which arranges them by the last race.

Sorted by the 4th last race

Horse	L	2L	3L	4L
Anonymous Guest	53.53	49.17	67.07	76.61
John Steed (IRE)	66.75	50.05	58.68	65.77
Rosenzoo (IRE)	64.88	68.33	58.09	62.98
Cogsworth	58.75	55.69	54.99	59.03
The Bitter Moose (IRE)	65.61	65.91	47.52	57.59
Alfred (FR)	59.38	64.27	66.6	53.92
Zariela	73	62.91	57.6	0

Sorted by the 3rd last race

Horse	L	2L	3L	4L
Anonymous Guest	53.53	49.17	67.07	76.61
Alfre (FR)	59.38	64.27	66.6	53.92
JohnSteed (IRE)	66.75	50.05	58.68	65.77
Rosenzoo (IRE)	64.88	68.33	58.09	62.98
Zariela	73	62.91	57.6	0
Cogsworth	58.75	55.69	54.99	59.03
TheBitter Moose (IRE)	65.61	65.91	47.52	57.59

Speed Ratings

Sorted by the 2nd last race

Horse	L	2L	3L	4L
Rosenzoo (IRE)	64.88	68.33	58.09	62.98
The Bitter Moose (IRE)	65.61	65.91	47.52	57.59
Alfred (FR)	59.38	64.27	66.6	53.92
Zariela	73	62.91	57.6	0
Cogsworth	58.75	55.69	54.99	59.03
John Steed (IRE)	66.75	50.05	58.68	65.77
Anonymous Guest	53.53	49.17	67.07	76.61

Sorted by the last race

Horse	L	2L	3L	4L
Zariela	73	62.91	57.6	0
John Steed (IRE)	66.75	50.05	58.68	65.77
The Bitter Moose (IRE)	65.61	65.91	47.52	57.59
Rosenzoo (IRE)	64.88	68.33	58.09	62.98
Alfred (FR)	59.38	64.27	66.6	53.92
Cogsworth	58.75	55.69	54.99	59.03
Anonymous Guest	53.53	49.17	67.07	76.61

I noticed Zariela in this race because in her last race she was top-rated, and her price looked inflated. To find if a horse is improving or not, I list the runners from 4th last race to the last race to see if they continually climb the table. Now this is not an exact science as some horse's fourth last race may have been last season or at least some time ago but that does not really matter. This showed that in comparison to others in the race Zariela was improving getting better with each race finishing top of the table on her last race.

Speed Ratings

however, that could be due to her last race being a 54K Class 2 race. She only actually climbed the table in her last three races as she had only run three times. Zariela did not win but she finished a close 2nd, 4 lengths clear of the rest of the field her price of 15/2 was very good value indeed.

When you do this some horses will jump up and down the table. It is worth leaving them well alone we are looking for consistency.

You do of course need to pick your races carefully relying on Speed Figures alone is not the way forward. They are an aid with other characteristics that must be considered. You may want to take Ratings into account or as I do pay considerable attention to trainer comments and form. Also watch the races of the horses you are interested in to see if they could have done better with a clear run go for quality not quantity.

When looking for improving horses they do not have to finish top of the table. As long as they are improving, and I would say get in the first four they could be worth a second look. I tend not to worry too much about the fourth last race if there is progression in the last three races. I leave horses alone that are first close to the top then drop down then up and down again. In other words, irregular performances as they tend to be risky selections. You may think you have done all your homework and for some inexplicable reason the horse just does not perform as expected. Well horses are like that they are not machines. I stick to selections that are making steady progress that is where the value is.

I can demonstrate what I mean by that by running through the race outlined on the following page.

Wed 20th Sep 2023

4.00 Beverley (9 runners)

Blue Sky Event Services Handicap

5f (1100 yards)

Speed Ratings

The speed figures for this race are on the following page. The 7/2 favourite Ey Up its Maggie is the overall top rated on speed figures. On her fourth last race, she is 2nd from bottom on SF. Her last three races are in the table. Also look at the positions of Count Dorsay and Mattice. I have deleted the bottom rated horse in each case due to space on the page.

Look how the favourite Ey up its Maggie who was bottom on her fourth last run moves up and down the table. Mattice who starts off eighth in table moves quickly up to being 2nd last time out. Count Dorsay moves more slowly up the table to finish top. Also notice as I will mention a few times in this book Ey up its Maggie is a Mare. Mattice and Count Dorsay are Geldings. For me Ey up its Maggie was a significant risk in this race. There is little between Mattice who rose quickly up the table and Count Dorsay both trained by Tim Easterby.

Speed Ratings

Horse	L	2L	3L	4L
Count Dorsay (IRE)	72.68	75.08	65.12	78.92
Mattice	72.08	66.31	54.39	86.76
Digital (IRE)	71.28	62.72	30	48.56
Ey Up Its Maggie	68.96	61.76	70.56	60.68
Motawaazy	64.49	59.09	60.9	62.09
Sound Reason	62.07	68.48	58.16	91
Prospect	61.8	60.56	73.08	68.17
May Blossom	55.48	68.44	66	68.12

Horse	L	2L	3L	4L
Star Of Lady M	55.19	84.11	55.92	67.29
Count Dorsay (IRE)	72.68	75.08	65.12	78.92
Sound Reason	62.07	68.48	58.16	91
May Blossom	55.48	68.44	66	68.12
Mattice	72.08	66.31	54.39	86.76
Digital (IRE)	71.28	62.72	30	48.56
Ey Up Its Maggie	68.96	61.76	70.56	60.68
Prospect	61.8	60.56	73.08	68.17

Horse	L	2L	3L	4L
Prospect	61.8	60.56	73.08	68.17
Ey Up Its Maggie	68.96	61.76	70.56	60.68
May Blossom	55.48	68.44	66	68.12
Count Dorsay (IRE)	72.68	75.08	65.12	78.92
Motawaazy	64.49	59.09	60.9	62.09
Sound Reason	62.07	68.48	58.16	91
Star Of Lady M	55.19	84.11	55.92	67.29
Mattice	72.08	66.31	54.39	86.76

Speed Ratings

The result of the race is shown below

1st Mattice 9/2
2nd Count Dorsay 9/2
3rd May Blossom 10/1
4th Ey Up Its Maggie 7/2Fav

There was only a short Head splitting the first two.
Ey Up Its Maggie was a further 2.5 lengths adrift. May Blossom for
a Filly also ran a sound race, but she too was erratic in the tables.
Just a word of warning here and this is something you may want to
study. If you check tables like this often enough you will notice that
Mares and Fillies can be unreliable. They jump up and down the
tables with regular monotony. However, when they have been near
the top then dropped down, they generally bounce back. Depending
on the days since they last ran of course. For me it is an unexplored
area but there could be very good value in doing that study.

There was a case like that on the same day at Beverley in the 5:10
race. Dandys Angel a Mare was top of the table then in her Last
Race she dropped to fifth then came and won her race at 9/2.

On the same day at Sandown Trust Rusty another Mare was the
top of the table in her 3rd last race. Then bottom in her second last
race then top in her last race. In this current race she finished last at
7/2.
This pattern is only recognisable in Handicaps in Maiden and
Novice races you need a complete different set of tools. There is
much less form to go on. Also, some Handicaps where you may
have a number of horses that have run in three Maidens or Novice
events. Something could and often do sprout new legs in their first
Handicap Race. Seasoned followers of the sport will know exactly
what I mean.

Speed Ratings

In the chapter on Ratings remember we talked about Hartswood winning at 8/1. On the same card speed ratings also had a field day. Not by the top rated overall the top rated in their last race won six of the eight races at the following prices.
11/8, 8/1, 13/2, 7/2, 11/4, and 4/1.
The last race speed rating is critical to be a decent one. Be careful early in the season and late in the season that the good Speed Rating is not coming from National Hunt Racing. You cannot mix the two figures.

In the chapter on Ratings, we looked at Speed figures from a different angle. That is the speed figure clocked last time out in comparison to the weight carried. In that chapter we looked at a horse top rated then compared the speed figure. Of course, the horse does not have to be top in the ratings table. For this exercise let us ignore the ratings table altogether.

07/10/2023 Newmarket Class 4 £5k the speed ratings for this race are shown on the opposite page.
These days I do not normally put too much work in for racing on a Saturday. Going back a few years I would look forward to Saturdays with relish. Saturday's racing is an excellent source of winners for the future. as I will explain in the chapter Days of The Week.

Whilst flicking through the races for the day, I noticed that Hand of God was top rated on speed. I remember watching his previous race when Cambridge won at Salisbury. I checked back again on that race. The Sporting Life replays showed all the runners for that day in the paddock. I thought Hand Of God still looked like he still had a bit of condition to work on. Despite the commentator saying how well he looked. I had also noticed that all of Roger Charlton's recent winners were taking 3-4 races before winning.

Speed Ratings

Horse	Rating	Odds	L	2L
Sisyphean	69.59	5/2	66.26	76.26
Hand Of God	67.59	9/1	70	55.53
Wonder	67.17	5/1	67.8	66.38
Kings Fountain	66.58	9/4	66.58	0
Purefoy	65.11	28/1	65.11	0
Dark VIper	62.66	50/1	63.83	60.3
Brave Call	59.81	50/1	59.81	0
Classic Encounter (Ire)	51.45	9/2	51.45	0
Ardara Rose (Ire)	47.86	200/1	47.86	0

Hand Of God was now on his third race he improved considerably from his 2nd last to his last race. He was already top speed rated in his last race if he improved again, he was going to take an awful lot of beating, Being forecast at 14/1 he looked a solid E/W bet. Unfortunately, he opened at 15/2. I was already concerned about Classic Encounter as Charlie Appleby's horses were running out of their Skin with 32% winners in the last 14 days, I really was not too concerned by too many of the others including Sisyphean the forecast favourite. It would be difficult to see Hand Of God not finishing in the frame here. He eventually drifted out to 9/1 after being at 6/1 for a while as the money poured in on other runners.

You can see from the last two ratings how much Hand Of God Improved from his 1st race to his 2nd race. If he does the same again today an E/W bet is nailed on.
Hand Of God went on to win Comfortably from Classic Encounter who will likely improve and find a race before the end of the season.

Speed Ratings

If I flick through speed ratings for the day, I look for something that stands out in the horse's last race. Either a rating that is out of line with the horse's position in the table or just an exceptional rating, Again I say watch that the rating has not come from a National Hunt race as that gives inflated ratings when compared to the flat or the All Weather. I then look to see if there is any justification for a rating higher than the rest of the field the majority of the time, I cannot find any justification for it. Or I find that if I adjust for weight carried this time it negates the advantage they had.

Then I came across the 7:00 at Wolverhampton a Class 5 £4K race table below.

Horse	Rating	L	2L
Mokaatil	82.98	77.51	57.56
El Hombre	80.15	67.75	71.68
Belle Fourche	76.82	66.88	55.21
Mellys Flyer	75.85	70.21	72.98
Regal Envoy	72.14	87.16	75.36
Kessaar Power	70.75	61.35	72.67
How Impressive	69.27	70.32	80.87
Fifty Year Storm	69.21	69.95	61.39
Beauzon	68.83	56.43	66.51
Some Nightmare	68.09	69.36	58.41
The Princess Poet	63.48	67.39	53.1

Speed Ratings

There is clearly a standout rating here that needs looking at. Why has Regal Envoy got a rating that is 10pts above the top-rated horse who is the nearest to him in their last race. Regal Envoy only carried 8-11 that day the time was fast. It was Regal Envoy that cut out the running and fought back well when headed. Ridden again today by a determined 7lb claimer in Wilkie Brandon. Today he will carry 9-2 the concern I did have was that W J Knight has not had a winner in twenty seven races. However, it was Regal Envoy who last won for him. As before I created a table from each horses last rating and the difference in pounds carried today. This is not an exact science but it one I like to use. See table below.

Horse	L	lbs difference	New Rating
Mokaatil	77.51	+15	62
El Hombre	67.75	+3	64
Belle Fourche	66.88	-4	70
Mellys Flyer	70.21	+2	68
Regal Envoy	87.16	+5	82
Kessaar Power	61.35	+7	54
How Impressive	70.32	+1	69
Fifty Year Storm	69.95	-2	72
Beauzon	56.43	-9	65
Some Nightmare	69.36	+9	60
The Princess Poet	67.39	=	67

Speed Ratings

You can see that Regal Envoy is still well clear of the rest and the gutsy way he ran last time he really does stand out here. By the way he was also top in the ratings table.

Result
1st Regal Envoy 9/1
2nd How Impressive 11/10 Fav
3rd Belle Fourche 11/1

Regal Envoy won by 2.75 lengths and was never headed despite the odd race comments that he was headed inside the final furlong. Whoever wrote that in the race comments must have been watching another race. Wilkie Brandon is a jockey to keep an eye on while still claiming 7lb.

Favourites

Favourites

No book about selecting horses as an investment potential would be complete without mentioning favourites. Horseracebase gives us thousands of ways for us to analyse favourites.

Let us start right at the low end of the market. Horses starting at odds-on up to even money. Some trainers have a poor record for horses starting at prices below even money. I hear so much chat on the course like "the trainer is fiddling, the jockey pulled the horse etc" it is just total rubbish. If you list out from whatever criteria you like whether it be flat, NH, or the All Weather any criteria of runners, race type, track, UK, or Ireland.

List all the trainers and then sort them by profit/loss you will always find the top trainers have the biggest loss for horses starting less than even money. The reason for that is bookmakers quite rightly believe they have the best quality horses and they do not want to take a significant risk with their runners. They automatically go to the head of the forecast market. Some punters wade in just because they have a short priced horse from a top stable. It does not seem to matter if they have the best form in the race.

As I have said before. I have a friend who makes a very good living backing horses at less than even money. Now he has certain parameters that he looks for obviously he does not invest on every horse starting at less than even money as that is a very quick way to the poor house. I cannot divulge all his secrets for betting at such short prices. One thing he must do is avoid betting on the top trainer's horses when they are clearly false favourites.

Like everything else you need to do your homework on trainers avoid top trainers at very short prices. What they do is give you value for money about other runners. That is the part of the market I would be looking at to take advantage of the better prices that naturally occur.

Favourites

In Ireland, the O'Brien's are obviously the top trainers they get a high percentage of winners. If you followed all their horses that start favourite, you will lose money every year. Now that statistic should tell you that their horses like the top trainers in the UK are not fair value for money. It should also tell you that others in the race could be very good value for money, with Horseracebase it is possible to weed some of these out.

Just let me mention there is a difference between a false favourite and a poor value for money favourite. A false favourite is a horse that is starting favourite but really does not deserve that position in the market. A poor value for money favourite is a horse that deserves to be at the top of the market, but the price is far too short for his chance of winning. These two situations happen every single day in both the UK and Ireland. For those of us who still have a living memory of days before the Exchanges appeared on the scene will remember the extortionate over rounds the bookmakers worked to. Usually around 130% or more in some cases. These days thanks to the exchanges the over round in favour of the bookmakers has been reduced significantly. The Exchanges show the over round at the head of their pages on every race by the time of the race it is often down to about 101% to 102% Plus sites like Odds Checker take all bookmakers into calculation to produce an overall figure you would need an account with every bookmaker to take advantage of that. I do not intend to tell you where you invest your money that is entirely up to you. My own feelings are that Bet 365 always offer good prices. Betfred is also up their with some of the fairer bookmakers. There are certain bookmakers both online and in the high street that do not offer fair value for money the majority of the time.

Screenshot of Non Hcp favs at BF prices over 11 years

Odds (BFSP)	Bets	Wins	Win%	P/L(SP)	Race%	P/L(BF)
1.01-1.25	15	14	93.33%	1.41	93.33%	1.74
1.26-1.5	172	124	72.09%	-2.63	72.09%	-2
1.51-1.75	335	213	63.58%	1.98	63.58%	7.74
1.76-2	496	251	50.60%	-43.5	50.60%	-35.09
2.01-2.25	533	230	43.15%	-71.72	43.15%	-57.88
2.26-2.5	579	249	43.01%	-18.19	43.23%	-3.04
2.51-2.75	582	216	37.11%	-46.11	37.31%	-33.2
2.76-3	671	239	35.62%	-17.71	35.94%	-6.3
3.01-3.5	953	324	34%	25.03	35.45%	63.4
3.51-4	857	233	27.19%	-52.37	28.73%	-20.87
4.01-4.5	449	111	24.72%	-20.35	26.62%	4.94
4.51-5	264	60	22.73%	-6.53	24.29%	8.83
5.01-5.5	147	33	22.45%	5.49	26.40%	19.16
5.51-6	73	16	21.92%	8.5	26.23%	15.04
6.01-7	38	8	21.05%	4.5	25.81%	11.08
7.01-8	2	0	0%	-2	0%	-2

The table above shows the returns of non-handicap favourites in The UK on the flat over an eleven year period the odds are at Betfair starting prices. You can easily see in the highlighted column that if you backed all the favourites in non-handicaps over the eleven-year period at BF odds of 3.01 or greater you would have made a profit of £99.58 below that price you would have made a loss of -£123.03. Remember these are decimal odds therefore 3.01 equates to a fraction over 2/1. The figures are also based on a £1 stake and 5% reduction for commission.

Favourites

Form	Horse	Jockey	Trainer	Odds
4512	Mountain Warrior	Rodriguez, Callum	Bethell, Ed	5/2f
Bethell, Ed (Trainer Notes) Excellent trainer, wins mdns either 2nd or 3rd time out, keeps them in same class, winners often go on to better things, can never be written off.				
261210	Quintus Arrius (IRE)	Doyle, James	Ryan, K A	9/2
Ryan, K A (Trainer Notes) Horses run often and win in their turn drop-in class helps, Normally finds a race for his maidens within first three races.				
2320323	Thankuappreciate	Scott, Rowan	Tinkler, N	9/2
Tinkler, N (Trainer Notes) Horses are showing a massive improvement on their 2nd run from a break.				

In the above race on the 5th August 2023, none of the first three in the market met the comments of their respective trainers. they were the first three in the betting market. they finished 4th, 5th and 7th in a seven runner race, showing that trainer comments can be very useful in determining whether a horse is value for money or not. If I am investing on a favourite I like to know that the horse is in line with the trainers current form and methods.

Favourites

	Form	Horse	Trainer	Odds
	7441	Without Flaw (IRE)	Watson, Archie	10/11

Watson Archie (Trainer Notes) 18% winners prolific place getter can improve horses taken over from other trainers. All horses on their 2nd or 3rd run need to be looked at very closely. Even if moved up in class particularly top class on 3rd run from break.

	6352	Tiora	Owens, Patrick	11/2

Owens, Patrick (Trainer Notes) Decent trainer, when he gets a win with a 2yo or 3yo tends to jump them too high and just fails, needs more checking.

	655	Fistral Beach (IRE)	Scott, George	13/2

Scott, George (Trainer Notes) 16% winners overall, one to be watched and checked. September 22 still ok'ish, 1st run 3%, if he runs a 2yo in a higher-class race first time out, then he thinks something of it, watch when dropped in class. Horses can maintain their form if kept to same class.

	575	Carnaby Princess	Easterby, T D	11/1

Easterby,T D (Trainer Notes) Horses can be well beaten in 3 maidens, then dropped in class for 1st hcp and win at a decent price, You really have to take note of Tim's horses being dropped in class and prize money, even if finishing last in a bigger race, often win or run well at big prices.

Favourites

PRE-RACE ANALYSIS: The table on the previous page is taken from a Nursery race run on 5th August 2023. I have omitted a number of columns of information due to space. From the four trainer comments alone, which horse would you rather your money on. At the time of writing this race has not been run there are ten runners. I have only taken the first four as a test and demonstration based on trainer's comments alone. Knowing nothing about previous form, dates class of race prize money etc, **Carnaby Princess** would be the choice, due the fact that this is her first run in handicap company after three runs in maiden company.

There are other factors at play here which currently you do not have the information for, there are also quite a few columns missing from the analysis. Which would help you make a decision. **Without Flaw** won a class 6 £3K race unchallenged on a Monday, I will tell you the significance of that later. **Tiora** was second in a class 6 £4K race at Nottingham. Nottingham is used by many trainers to bring decent horses on, that could be very reliable form. **Fistral Beach** was beaten 7.3 lengths in class 4 £5K race at Bath. **Carnaby Princess** was beaten 11.5 lengths in a class 5 £5K race at Ripon. Given that added information does that change your mind. For me it is between **Carnaby Princess** who we think will improve because of the information written about the trainer, and **Tiora**, with **Tiora** getting the nod on the information given.

POST-RACE ANALYSIS: now we know the result, First **Tiora** 7/2, second **Fistral Beach** 6/1, third 16/1 shot not mentioned above. Fourth was **Carnaby Princess** 13/2. The 7/4 favourite **Without Flaw** was fifth. I can go into depth as to why Without Flaw was a very poor Favourite there was no Value for Money there. The result of this race was deciphered quite easily with information entirely available on Horseracebase.

There is a misconception that Favourites worldwide win 30% of the time. Yes, it is close to that figure. Over the last 5 years overall Favourites in the UK have won 32.5% of the time and in Ireland 29.7% of the time. The breakdown of that is in non-handicaps they have won 39.3% of the time and in Handicaps they have won 27.8% of the time.

The breakdown between UK and Ireland is that for non-handicaps in the UK they win 40% of the time and in Ireland they win 37.8% of the time. The big void comes in Handicaps UK 29%, Ireland 21.8% set out in the table below.

Favourites over a five year period	Handicaps	Non Handicaps
All	27.8%	39.3%
UK	29%	40%
Ireland	21.8%	37.8%

The above figures show it is more difficult to predict the winner in Ireland than it is in the UK the reason for the difference is purely down to the number of runners per race. The average number or runners per race in Ireland is 11.01 where the average number of runners in the UK is 8.32. The difference for runners in handicaps is that the average number in the UK is 9.2 and in Ireland it is 13.6, and for Non-Handicaps the Numbers are 10.63 for Ireland and 8.6 for the UK. These numbers may seem meaningless to some. However, they have a bearing on your chances of continual finding winners. The ideal scenario is to break down Favourites to runners. The less runners the better your chances whether you are a favourite backer or not. The following table breaks down the number of winning Favourites in comparison to runners in both Handicaps and Non-Handicaps.

Favourites

Number of runners	Winning Fav % Hcps	Winning Fav% Non Hcps
2	50%	77.78%
3	51%	53.45%
4	40%	51.68%
5	39.75%	51.21%
6	34.84%	40.48%
7	30.77%	44.17%
8	30.57%	37.28%
9	28.45%	35.94%
10	26.64%	38.1%
11	22.75%	37.79%
12	24.64%	37.15%
13	24.4%	33.56%
14	22.63%	33.04%
15	20.21%	30.56%
16	17.65%	28.14
17	18%	31.18
18	15.74%	33.33%
19	17.5%	27.27%
20	15.63%	25%

Favourites

The preceding table shows the vast differences between backing favourites in handicaps to non-handicaps. In non-handicaps favourites are still winning over 30% of the time right up to 18 runners. Where in handicaps they only win up to 30% of the time up to 8 runners. For favourite backers that is vital information because for both handicaps and non-handicaps the larger the field the larger the starting price has the potential to be.

I know that many people like to follow favourites. You can through HRB list out trainers in many ways. If you list out say all trainers over the last 10 years that have made a profit at SP you will find it is the smaller trainers that make the profit. The larger well-known trainers lose a considerable amount of money if you were to follow their favourite runners blindly. The tables shown on the next two pages show the top profit-making trainers in the UK & Ireland.

Though the tables tell a story as to which trainers to follow. They are of course historical what has happened in the past is no guarantee that the same will happen in the future. As far as the trainers listed in the tables are concerned if you list these out for yourself in HRB it is the fact that top trainer's favourites show a considerable loss that is more important. As that also tells you that top trainer's horses are at a false price, and you should never be concerned about siding against them.

Just as a comparison the average win% of the trainer's in the table is 37.15%, the average win% of trainers at the bottom of the table which are the bigger trainers is 31.07%, what you could take from this is that if you are analysing a race and the favourite is from a smaller stable the price is more likely to be of value than if the horse comes from a leading trainer.

Favourites

Irish Trainers whose horses when starting favourite have made the most profit at SP over the last ten years, on the flat.

Criteria	Win%	P/L(SP)	P/L(BF)
Fahey, Jarlath P	41.38	23	30.41
Slattery, Andrew	33.33	19.81	26.85
Lupini, Miss Natalia	34.29	19.58	27.09
Fahey, Peter	38.1	19.38	23.07
Marnane, David	34.29	19.23	21.35
Twomey, P	43.07	17.06	25.9
Doyle, Timothy	50	15.88	18.06
Quinn, J J	66.67	14	15.92
ODonnell, P F	50	13.83	16.39
Fahey, R A	40	10.3	13.95
Duffy, S M	75	9.5	10.93
Doyle, Eoin	62.5	9	9.91
Midgley, P T	50	8.5	9.28
Downey, P	50	8.5	9.47
Cody, Patrick	44.44	8.5	11.36
Byrne, Philip Michael	50	8.08	8.81
Martin, A J	27.16	7.93	17.34

Favourites

UK Trainers whose horses when starting favourite have made the most profit at SP over the last ten years on the flat.

Criteria	Win%	P/L(SP)	P/L(BF)
Wall, C F	42.04	56.7	65.65
Burke, K R	36.03	45.56	74.76
Williams, Ian	33.2	32.11	45.67
Millman, B R	33.63	27.67	39.35
Easterby, M W	29.34	27.18	42.07
Menuisier, David	36.45	25.18	32.92
Carroll, A W	33.33	23.63	40.38
Chapple-Hyam, P W	45.78	23.59	28.82
West, Adam	46.67	21.06	24.27
Alston, E J	30.77	17.84	22.65
Ellison, B	34.27	16.96	28.22
Mason, Christopher	39.29	16.33	20.46
Tinkler, N	29.28	15.62	28.52
Brown, A D	54.55	14.63	16.85
Carr, Mrs R A	26	14.47	31.97
Whitaker, R M	28.95	13	16.5
Frost, Kevin	39.29	12.41	14.56

Favourites

HRB lets you list out horses that have either drifted or shortened in the market. It is a widespread belief that horses that shorten in the market have a better chance because of stable confidence. I have looked at this from various angles and though when you get down to short prices a slight shortening movement does win slightly more often than a slight drifting movement. The movement out actually makes more profit no matter where you look at it on the scale. The moral of this story is that if your horse drifts in the market you should rejoice because if you are on Best Odds in the long term, you are better off.

If you are well into your favourites, then the following Stats should be familiar to you I would hope. If not, they do make interesting reading.

The following stats are for all horses in the UK and Ireland listed separately that started favourite over the last 20 years. I have broken the percentages down to sex of the horse as they do perform differently. The first data is from non-handicap races only

Breakdown of favourite winning percentages in Non-Handicaps in Flat races on turf, over a 20 year period

Criteria	Bets	Wins	Win% UK	Win% Ireland
Colts	9701	3918	40.2	40.96
Horses	259	103	38.12	50
Geldings	3965	1555	40.02	37.03
Fillies	7912	3001	38.46	36.7
Mares	324	130	36.81	44.37

Both sets of data for the UK and Ireland show similar figures they both show that Females are slightly less dependable than the males.

Favourites

The surprising thing is though the data in relation to Colts and Fillies is quite small how much better the percentages are in Ireland for both Horses and Mares.

The table below also over a Twenty-year period shows the reliability of the sexes on the All Weather courses, in non-handicaps

Criteria	Bets	Wins	Win% UK	Win% Ireland
Colts	3576	1596	44.54	45.25
Horses	90	41	46.51	25
Geldings	3359	1424	42.81	40
Fillies	3290	1325	40.18	40.87
Mares	147	54	37.5	33.33

Again, we can see that the Males of the species perform better than the female. We can ignore the 25% for Horses in Ireland as the data is too small just 1 from 4 as for reliability with your favourite selections the Approximate 4-5% in favour of the males may well be crucial at the end of the day,

Now let us look at the same data for handicap races Again over a twenty-year period. First of all, Flat turf racing.

Criteria	Bets	Wins	Win% UK	Win% Ireland
Colts	5160	1482	29.12	25.74
Horses	127	32	25.41	20
Geldings	22918	6063	27.28	21.35
Fillies	8831	2419	28.68	21.61
Mares	1992	545	28.39	24.18

Favourites

Again, there is a slight difference in Males and females. More so in Ireland let us look at handicaps on All-Weather courses.

Criteria	Bets	Wins	Win% UK	Win% Ireland
Colts	2657	875	33.09	30.81
Horses	159	54	34.44	25
Geldings	16728	4783	28.98	25.27
Fillies	4411	1251	29.14	21.2
Mares	1077	273	26.03	21,38

Again, there is a remarkable difference between the two sexes in Ireland there is a 9% difference between Colts and Fillies. Something well worth considering when you are thinking of investing. I have not been All Weather racing in Ireland yet. maybe the kick Back from the artificial surface is greater? I am not sure.

You could break this favourites data down in hundreds of ways. It is worth looking at the class of race that each perform in though.

The table below shows how Colts perform in all classes in the UK again in Non-Handicap races on the flat.

Criteria	Bets	Wins	Win% UK
Class 1	1342	497	37.03
Class 2	370	130	35.14
Class 3	447	167	37.36
Class 4	1980	749	37.83
Class 5	2987	1324	44.33
Class 6	197	77	39.09

Favourites

It is worth noting how much better the colts perform in the lower classes. Of course, you can do this with all the sexes, and it may well be worth your time doing just that. In Handicap races it is a similar picture though the improved percentages kick in around class 3 being 30% winners and Class 4 being 32% winners it is worth getting these small percentages in your favour.

If I have a selection and I think the filly could be the best in the race. Could be the best, is not good enough as the percentages will be against you. I like to know if I am investing in a filly she is on top of her game and other factors are in her favour.

The breakdown for Geldings is even greater as there is 7% difference in Geldings winning Class 2= 32%. Geldings that start favourite and win in class 5= 39%. You could look at these in two ways as I have mentioned before. If you are a favourite backer stick to races where they have the highest win percentage. Or where the favourite has a low win percentage to see if there is anything in the race that could mount a serious challenge. The Latter would be my preference.

Horses that won last time out in either Handicaps or Non-Handicaps whether they were favourite or are favourite this time only win around 17% of the time. That is obvious as some run against each other they cannot all win. This is another list of trainers that I keep. Those that can achieve this greater than 20% of the time and trainers that only achieve it less than 12% of the time. Of which there are a great many.

On the following page I have produced the winning favourites Month by Month for the UK and Ireland. You can see that June and July are by far the better months for winning Favourites. Yet for Ireland the number of placing favourites is better in the lower Months. They may not win but they do still place that is worth bearing in mind.

Favourites

If you are a favourite backer, you want to bare the following table in mind. The best months of the year for backing favourites are June and July as can be seen by the following table for 2023. the reason there has been so few favourites for November is that it has been an extremely wet month, with plenty of cancellations.

Winning Flat Favourites in the UK Month by Month for 2023

Criteria	Bets	Wins	Win%	Place%
April	307	83	27.04	51.47
May	647	212	32.77	59.97
June	743	253	34.05	60.03
July	692	236	34.1	61.85
August	708	213	30.08	58.62
September	602	183	30.4	56.15
October	283	78	27.56	59.01
November	21	6	28.57	52.38

Winning Flat Favourites in Ireland Month by Month for 2023

Criteria	Bets	Wins	Win%	Place%
March	24	11	45.83	62.5
April	100	29	29	61
May	152	36	23.68	47.37
June	174	58	33.33	57.47
July	189	67	35.45	59.26
August	171	49	28.66	62.57
September	188	53	28.19	64.36
October	117	32	27.35	59.83
November	8	1	12.5	87.5

Race Courses

Race Courses

I am constantly being asked if there are any courses to avoid or are there any courses that I would not go to. The answer to that is "No" the more courses you go to the better feel you get for the sport. Going to the course for me is necessary. I must admit I have not yet travelled to all the Irish courses. It is on my bucket list for the next two years to fill that dream.

These days I mainly go to courses where I can see the horses in the pre parade ring. Usually by the time they get to the main parade ring especially flat horses and 2yo's in particular. They are beginning to get quite keen and are no longer relaxed. Whilst in the pre parade ring horses in general are more relaxed and it is easier to see their true confirmation. One of the few exceptions I would make to that would be Haydock. I love going to Haydock both as a venue plus the visibility of the horses. if you have never been I suggest you do at least give Haydock a try.

This book is not about picking selections from the paddock that is another subject that I may touch on once or twice throughout this book. What I want to do here is show how you can make the study of courses, trainer's, and favourites profitable. Or at least see them in a different light.

I do keep banging on about using the data provided by Horseracebase to your advantage. I make no apologies for that. The systems and information you can obtain from Horseracebase is phenomenal. There are hundreds of thousands of diverse ways to interpret data to use to your advantage.

Let us look at courses throughout the UK and Ireland. Though I am not a massive follower of favourites. I use favourites in other ways. It is always useful to see how favourites fair in different circumstances then you can see if it is beneficial to look elsewhere for a selection.

Race Courses

There are several reasons why certain courses perform better for favourites than others. In the main they all revolve around the basic theory that favourites win around 30% of the time. For flat racing in the UK there is a 10% difference in the best and worst courses for winning favourites over a ten-year period. The course with the highest percentage of winners is Yarmouth with 36.44% winners the lowest is York with 26.71% of winners. York is also the bottom of the table when it comes to favourites placing with only 54.43%. The best course for placed favourites is Chepstow with 62.98% of favourites placing.

Why are some courses more successful for favourites than others? Let us look at York and Yarmouth and interrogate the differences. York is the worst return for favourites. With Horseracebase you can break down any data you care to name. Just looking at a comparison of the two courses on the following page the reason for the difference becomes obvious.

Yarmouth has a maximum of sixteen runners in the last ten years, where York holds races of up to twenty-two runners. The more runners there are the less chance the favourite has of winning consistently. That too can be shown in terms of percentages the interesting thing here is having a direct comparison between the number of runners and winning percentage of the favourites.

Yarmouth has a vast amount more races between 3 and 8 runners therefore the favourite has a higher percentage chance of winning. However, the greater the number of runners the more interesting things get.

For fourteen runners Yarmouth Favourites score approximately 11% more often than York for fifteen Runners the difference is around 20%. To me that would make me want to look beyond the favourite for a selection at York. You can break every course down to see how the favourite percentages work out then check handicaps to non-handicaps Check for distances too. The possibilities are endless.

Courses

Below is the breakdown of the two courses over the last ten-year period. The following page is over a twenty-one-year period just to capture more data.

York Winning Favourites					Yarmouth Winning Favourites			
Runners	Bets	Wins	Win%		Runners	Bets	Wins	Win%
3	2	2	100%		3	24	13	54.17%
4	17	10	58.82%		4	78	41	52.56%
5	40	20	50%		5	153	73	47.71%
6	72	27	37.50%		6	197	79	40.10%
7	88	38	43.18%		7	225	81	36%
8	106	34	32.08%		8	227	78	34.36%
9	117	36	30.77%		9	155	48	30.97%
10	114	35	30.70%		10	118	39	33.05%
11	97	22	22.68%		11	99	25	25.25%
12	85	21	24.71%		12	88	31	35.23%
13	80	21	26.25%		13	52	13	25%
14	67	12	17.91%		14	38	11	28.95%
15	74	12	16.22%		15	28	10	35.71%
16	50	9	18%		16	7	0	0%
17	54	10	18.52%					
18	67	13	19.40%					
19	80	13	16.25%					
20	56	6	10.71%					
21	15	2	13.33%					
22	18	4	22.22%					

Courses

Below are the numbers over a twenty-one-year period. Once again you can see that that Yarmouth has considerably more races with fewer runners. The real interesting point is from 12 to 20 runners where Yarmouth scores considerably higher than York.

York

Runners	Bets	Wins	Win%
3	3	3	100%
4	30	17	56.67%
5	87	38	43.68%
6	162	55	33.95%
7	191	69	36.13%
8	212	68	32.08%
9	210	57	27.14%
10	224	63	28.13%
11	208	55	26.44%
12	179	46	25.70%
13	151	40	26.49%
14	139	22	15.83%
15	141	29	20.57%
16	121	22	18.18%
17	115	25	21.74%
18	121	21	17.36%
19	162	31	19.14%
20	124	25	20.16%
21	19	3	15.79%
22	21	4	19.05%

Yarmouth

Runners	Bets	Wins	Win%
3	41	23	56.10%
4	127	70	55.12%
5	266	124	46.62%
6	377	146	38.73%
7	445	163	36.63%
8	413	139	33.66%
9	377	111	29.44%
10	286	85	29.72%
11	259	72	27.80%
12	212	65	30.66%
13	155	39	25.16%
14	134	42	31.34%
15	123	31	25.20%
16	64	13	20.31%
17	13	4	30.77%
18	9	0	0%
19	12	3	25%
20	18	6	33.33%

Courses

In the UK and Ireland, we have such a variety of courses Left Hand, Right Hand, Straight, Undulating, Flat, etc. that is what makes Racing here so interesting.

All Weather courses all show about the same percentage of favourite winners around 30-33%, no surprise there I suppose. There is just one that stands out. Chelmsford over 1M6F and 2M the favourites have won around 37% of the time over both distances.

The breakdown for the Irish courses is on the next page.

You can of course break down every course by distance of race too if we look at every course over 5 Furlongs then both Folkstone and Lingfield (Turf) both have winning percentages of 44.23% and 43.39% respectively. Unfortunately, Folkstone temporarily closed in 2012 to date there is no sign of it opening again.
43.39% for Lingfield favourites is exceptional they show a profit at SP on their own. Further analysis of the favourites over 5 furlongs could be very rewarding. non-handicap favourites have 55% record. Handicaps have a 31.71% record both show a profit at SP. The worst course over 5 furlongs for favourites is surprisingly Epsom with just 15.73% scoring. York has a very poor record with just 22.73% scoring. Remember when creating systems to do with percentages they are only an indication of past results they are no guarantee of future results. They are just a guide to be used with other selection methods.

Another point to bear in mind when considering a selection is the going. Over the last 10 years 36.4% of favourites have won on Firm going but only 29% on soft or heavy going. I will cover this again in the chapter on Going.

Courses

There is an 11% difference here between Downpatrick and Fairyhouse. An in-depth investigation as to why that is will be well worth while.

These percentages will change over the course of time as more data becomes available, the percentages given here need to be used in conjunction with other selection methods, but what they do is give you a starting point to develop systems to check out more Thoroughly.

Track	Bets	Wins	Win%	Track	Bets	Wins	Win%
Downpatrick	97	35	36.08%	Roscommon	721	217	30.10%
Clonmel	228	76	33.33%	Naas	1526	458	30.01%
Tipperary	1037	345	33.27%	Ballinrobe	440	132	30%
Tramore	352	115	32.67%	Sligo	448	133	29.69%
Wexford	259	83	32.05%	Galway	921	273	29.64%
Down Royal	622	197	31.67%	Navan	1224	357	29.17%
Leopardstown	2466	771	31.27%	Curragh	3326	965	29.01%
Bellewstown	539	168	31.17%	Listowel	567	163	28.75%
Limerick	695	215	30.94%	Cork	1142	325	28.46%
Killarney	782	241	30.82%	Tralee	120	32	26.67%
Gowran Park	1480	449	30.34%	Thurles	88	22	25%
Punchestown	43	13	30.23%	Fairyhouse	816	202	24.75%

Courses

28th September 2023 another day spent at Pontefract races and another day of surprises for me. It never ceases to amaze me that punters and connections of the horses never seem to cotton on that the stiff uphill at Pontefract saps the horse's strength massively when the going is anything softer than good. I ask you to watch the racing from this day and pay particular attention to the top weight in each race.

Only one Joint top weighted horse won today that was Beyond Borders who was the 2/1 fav. Beyond Borders looked a picture in the Pre-Parade Ring standing out above his rivals. Even he was being caught hand over fist at the death by the runner up, but he did at least prevail. No less than four top weighted favourites were turned over. Maybe the best example of how the Pontefract Hill effects horses that are made too much use of too early is in the 5:05 race. Dashing Panther was the 2/1 Fav carrying 10st 4lb.

I had Dashing Panther down as looking really well in the pre-Parade Ring. I also had Baltic who had done little prior to today as looking particularly strong. Baltic was carrying 8st 13lb. Dashing Panther made his move two furlongs out. A furlong out the legs were beginning to go under the hefty 10st 4lb. Baltic with his light weight was getting into top gear. Joe Fanning did well to keep Dashing Panther going again to hang on for second.

Ryan Rossa rode a treble in the first three races not including the first which was an apprentice race. Watch his positioning in each race just behind the leaders turning for home. The leaders heading for the furlong pole start to drop away. Almost every race has something coming from the gods at the death to make it a tight finish.
I have been going to Pontefract for more years than I care to remember. The same situation arises every time that the going is softer than good.

Courses

This is not just my theory it is backed up by data too, the table below is over a ten-year period at Pontefract on going that is either Good to Soft, Soft, or Heavy. The table shows the top six in the weight table in Handicaps. The second table shows the runners at Redcar which is flat under the exact same conditions.

Pontefract Win % of the Top weighted horse verses next 5			Redcar Win % of the Top weighted horse verses next 5		
Criteria	Races	Win%	Criteria	Races	Win%
Top Weight	274	11.31	Top Weight	298	13.09
2nd TW	219	13.24	2nd TW	269	7.43
3rd	235	13.62	3rd	247	9.31
4th	231	14.29	4th	229	7.86
5th	223	7.17	5th	257	10.89
6th	199	7.54	6th	240	7.92

At Pontefract, the top weighted horse in Handicaps does not win as often as the 2nd - 4th top weighted, whereas at a flat course like Redcar under the same conditions the top weighted horse wins much more often than the others listed. Remembering that the top weighted horse has presumably shown the best form to date therefore often starts as favourite.

Sometimes the top weighted horse may only be a lb or two above the rest that could also be data worth looking at which can also easily be done.

Courses

All the previous information may seem obvious with horses carrying weight uphill on soft ground it isn't the same for all courses with a steep uphill finish. For example, I have not witnessed the same on another course that I like to go to as often as possible which is Beverley. The table for Beverley under the same conditions is shown below. I have also compared it to Hamilton which is a great course to go to if you have never been.

Beverley Win % of the Top weighted horse verses next 5			Hamilton Win % of the Top weighted horse verses next 5		
Criteria	Races	Win%	Criteria	Races	Win%
Top Weight	235	20	Top Weight	528	12.31
2nd TW	202	15.35	2nd TW	457	12.04
3rd	203	14.29	3rd	442	17.65
4th	211	13.74	4th	446	13.68
5th	181	6.63	5th	406	11.58
6th	193	9.33	6th	417	12.47

Beverley shares much the same characteristics as Pontefract other than the fact one is right-handed, and the other is left-handed the climb to the finish is much the same.

At Beverley, the top weight on ground that is softer than good wins 20% of the time and the percentages fall away as you go down the weight chart. Which is what you would expect on most courses. At Hamilton, the numbers are very much the same down to the 6th top weighted horse. Again, the weight carried is influencing the higher weighted horses as you would expect the top weighted horse to win more often which is the case at most courses.

Courses

Just to prove the point let us look at the same courses on going that is described as Good or Good to Firm.

Pontefract Win % of the Top weighted horse verses next 5 on Good or Good to firm going.

Redcar Win % of the Top weighted horse verses next 5 on Good or Good to firm going.

Criteria	Races	Win%	Criteria	Races	Win%
Top Weight	613	16.15	Top Weight	647	14.99
2nd TW	508	13.19	2nd TW	538	13.01
3rd	527	14.04	3rd	530	9.62
4th	478	12.55	4th	520	10.96
5th	440	12.05	5th	540	10
6th	425	11.76	6th	491	9.78

Pontefract has gone up from 11.31% to 16.15%, whereas Redcar has also improved but marginally from 13.09% to 14.99%. there is a whole load of data that you can apply to all courses. It is worth the time putting in the work even if it just helps get a feel for the courses. There is nothing better than being on course and seeing all courses for yourself.

There is one thing that is common to some courses and not others that cannot be analysed by data, and that is the horse itself.

Courses

Irish Courses comparisons to top weighted horses.

Fairyhouse

Let us look at some of the Irish courses like Fairyhouse for example. Fairyhouse has not held a flat meeting on anything other than Good or Firm Ground in the last two years, over the preceding 8 years though Fairyhouse is relatively flat it does have a slight rise to the finish line. The top weight in Handicaps have won 13.68% of the time the data is a little scarce for Fairyhouse due to the small number of flat meetings however the numbers speak for themselves. Also, they are slightly misrepresented by a number of the top weights being rank outsiders. Taking the top 3 weights in handicap races 9.55% have won, of those ninety-six started as favourites of which only eighteen won. These are statistics that you should bear in mind when looking to invest in races.

Cork

Cork is an odd one as far as statistics are concerned as it is a relatively flat track but also fairly tight. The top weight in Good to soft and softer ground only win 6% of the time whereas horses that are 4th to 10th in the weight scale win 9.6% of the time collectively.

Killarney

Killarney is one of the fairest tracks for Favourites carrying top weight. Top Weights overall win 16.39% of the time with the top weighted Favourites winning 35.71% of the time and top weighted 2nd favourites winning 28.57% of the time. Third favourites that are carrying top weight win 20% of the time. Very few tracks have that percentage of horses carrying top weight in handicaps that are in the first three in the betting Market with a remarkable win record.

Courses

Roscommon

Roscommon is another very fair and kind track to the top weights with the outright top weighted horse winning 18% of the time, showing a healthy Level stake profit at SP. If the top weighted horse is in the first two in the betting market, they are showing a win percentage over 30% which is a remarkable statistic.

In the main tracks in Ireland are quite fair for the top weighted horses. The draw on some courses seems to be far more important and may have a bearing on the higher weighted horses. That study needs to be done and could generate some remarkably interesting angles.

I have said previously there is no substitute for being on the course and looking at the horses for yourself. I was at Pontefract recently and made a note of the horses that looked like they were fit and ready to run a very decent race. In the final race I made a note about Mersea a filly who looked particularly well in the paddock. She went off at 4/1 joint second favourite she got murdered on the turn for home by The Dunkirk Lads. It may be worth looking back at the race of that incident she was never going to get in the hunt from then on. She was still only beaten three lengths if she runs again in the near future, she may be better value than her price suggests. If I had not been at the course that day, I may not have given Mersia a second look next time out.

At courses like Pontefract, Beverley, Hamilton etc you need horses with strong quarters to power themselves up the hill when they are getting tired, light framed horses rarely win at these courses in the third race on the card Magico (a Gelding) and Zayina (a Filly) were vying for favouritism both at 2/1, Zayina ended up 6/5 Favourite. there was a vast difference between the two when viewed in the paddock Zayina is much more lightly built than Magico.

Courses

When viewed from behind as the two horses were walking away from the steps. You can get an extremely unobstructed view of their quarters off the steps at Pontefract it was clear that Magico had the muscle to carry him up the Pontefract Hill whereas Zayina, though looking extremely well in herself does not have the powerful quarters quite the same. Therefore, it was no surprise to see Magico come and out power Zayina close to home.

I see this sort of thing every time I am at one of these courses it not only gives me an edge on the course on the day. It is valuable information for when they next run depending on which course they run on.

09/10/2023

Another day and another meeting at Pontefract I am not happy that I cannot get to this meeting as the 2:00 race is fascinating as far as form is concerned. A 2yo race over 1m 2f. I looked at this race late last night fully expecting to come out thinking that Prepschool cannot get beaten in this. He is well clear in the ratings table and well clear in each of their last races in the speed figure table. I did what I always do and watched each of their preceding races. You really need to try to follow me on this I will try to explain my thinking on this race as clearly as possible. I could have put this race in any chapter in this book as it involves everything we have already covered. It involves Trainers, Ratings, Speed Ratings, Favourites and Courses plus it also involves watching previous races.

You really need to watch the previous race of the first three in the market here. Prepschool, The Hun and Curran in fact you only need to watch two races as The Hun finished second to the other two.

The Hun finished second to Prepschool in his first ever race, running on nicely at the finish when Prepschool had gone clear.

Courses

This was class 2 £15K race at Ripon. Part of my notes on The Hun's trainer read *"Maidens and Novices often can win 2nd time out; they can make a big improvement on their 2nd visit to a racecourse."*

I know that K R Burke does not like his young horses knocked about on their initial run which is quite right. There is nothing worse than seeing a young horse being punished in the final furlong. It does no good for the horse or for the sport. I personally hate to see it K R Burke leaves a bit to work on with his young horses therefore we can expect an improved run from The Hun when he runs again. Which he did on the 19/09/23 at Newcastle. This time in a class 5 £4K race over 1m 2f after a promising performance in Class 2 race he started as the 4/5 Favourite. This time he came across Curran a Charlie Johnston horse being dropped in class and prize money having its 2nd outing. We have already covered that scenario.

If you have watched each of the races you would have seen that Curran also beat The Hun comfortably but maybe not as comfortably as Prepschool did. Currently based on Ratings, Speed figures and both races Prepschool still has the edge.

Now here comes the crunch for me Prepschool's race was over 1m today's race is over 1m 2f an extra 2 furlongs is a long way for a 2yo. An extra two furlongs at Pontefract when the last 2 furlongs are uphill on Good to Soft ground will seem more like 3 furlongs to a young horse.

If you have watched the two races, watch them again watch Prepschool in the early part of his race. Daniel Tudhope struggles to keep him from tearing away for at least the first two furlongs he is fighting him all the way. Unless Prepschool has settled in the 51 days since he last ran, he is going to be flying out the gate at Pontefract as the first two furlongs will be downhill. By the time he hits the hill two furlongs from home he will have spent a massive amount of energy.

whereas Curran and The Hun are more relaxed in the early part of their races which will help them when they hit the hill at Pontefract.

	Horse	Total	Odds	LR
Ratings Odds as they were at 10:00am	Prepschool	217.4	10/11	117.0
	Curran	176.4	6/1	86.3
	The Hun	169.5	7/2	63.5
	Flavor	137.2	22/1	68.4
	Love Safari	110.1	10/1	50.7
	Synchronize (IRE)	94.3	9/1	43.2
	Cestrian Spirit(IRE)	89.0	100/1	40.2

	Horse	Rating	Odds	L
Speed Ratings Odds as they were at 10:00am	Prepschool	74.4	10/11	79.12
	The Hun	70.06	7/2	62.8
	Flavor	65.6	22/1	73.38
	Curran	63.02	6/1	64
	Love Safari	59.22	10/1	59.22
	Cestrian Spirit(IRE)	48.56	100/1	48.88
	Synchronize (IRE)	45.2	9/1	45.2

You can see from the two Tables above that if we just take Ratings and Speed Ratings alone then Prepschool is home and hosed. This is the point where I wish I were at the course to see each of these runners. As I have not seen any of these horses up close, I can only go from what I can see of them in their respective races.

Courses

Prepschool and Curran are of similar builds with Curran slightly more powerful in the neck. I really believe that Curran will out do Prepschool in the last furlong. However, Prepschool looks a lovely horse, and I am going to sit this one out. Without being on course this is too close to call I will watch the race with great deal of interest. I think The Hun's last race against Curran he was flat to the boards, he will need to improve to get close to the other two today.

I watched the race with more than my normal interest. I was shocked in the transformation of Preschool. David Egan had him settled in behind straight from the gates it was Curran who made the running pinched a length or two on the turn and just hung on from a strong finishing Prepschool and even a stronger finishing The Hun. It was a brilliant race in the last furlong I was glad I sat it out. these three horses are going to go on to better things. The Hun seems to be difficult to get into his stride but when he does get going, he will be very difficult to beat over 1m 4f as a three-year-old Providing he is on a course with a decent straight. It is interesting to note that the rest of the field were 15 lengths adrift of the front three.

Courses

This is why I keep saying you need to do your homework to be honest Preschool was far too short for me. Even if that were not the case I would not have invested in this race as it was too close to call if in doubt leave out.

I dare say that if I was into place betting Curran would have been a great investment, I do not know at this time what his place price was. these are the sort of races that place investors should be looking at.

There are plenty of sites on the Internet these days that describe details of courses their characteristics, the draw advantage etc, the best way to learn about courses is to actually go to the races if possible. Keep a note of everything good and bad about the course including access and Egress, I love going to Newmarket but the free for all of egressing out of the course car park is an absolute shamble. You arrive with Car Park attendants telling you where to go etc everything is well organised. Leaving you are left to the mercy of the crowd. There are other courses that work in the same way with a bottle neck at the one exit gate. I made notes of all these courses in the past but as I have been to them so many times, I know which courses I should be leaving before the last race and which ones it is worth stopping to watch the last race.

There is a book on the market that covers every course in the UK and Ireland which encourages you to take notes of the courses you visit. It is certainly on sale at Amazon and maybe elsewhere called "Travelling the Turf Notebook" Alternatively just keep your own notes in a diary.

Day of the Week

Day of week

Another well underestimated area to look at when evaluating form is what day of the week did the form you are evaluating happen. Let me explain with some data analysis from Horseracebase, we established earlier that fewer favourites win on a Saturday than any other day of the week. Looking at the table on the following page taking horses that won on a Saturday in a Handicap. In their last race in Class 3,4 or 5 race then reappeared on a Saturday again. The second table shows the results of that.

Only 15.4% win again on a Saturday. That is an extremely low percentage in comparison to returning on other days of the week. there are of course reasons for that. Firstly, the win in a Handicap would have resulted in a penalty or the next time out they could be going for a higher-class race. Those variables are again easy to break down.

The third table shows the results of horses under the same conditions but won on a Monday.

The Saturday winners win again on average 18.1% of the time. The Monday winners win next time out on average 16.4% of the time. When we are playing with minor percentages that is a considerable difference.

I must stress at this point this data is for flat racing only. All Weather racing has different outcomes.

Another interesting fact is that if you take the winners of a class 1 or 2 race on a Saturday. They will win again next time out an average of 30% of the time. Yet winners of class 1 or 2 race on any other day of the week only win on average 20% of the time next time out. These are form lines well worth considering when evaluating form.

The following table shows horses that won on a Saturday at either Ascot, Chester, Newmarket, Sandown, York, or Nottingham, how they faired next time out on given days.

Day of the Week

Saturday winners next
time out average 18.1%

Criteria	Bets	Wins	Win%
Sunday	366	73	19.95
Monday	494	91	18.42
Tuesday	405	78	19.26
Wednesday	470	89	18.94
Thursday	632	112	17.72
Friday	1014	170	16.77
Saturday	1168	180	15.51

Monday winners next
time out average 16.4%

Criteria	Bets	Wins	Win%
Sunday	298	35	11.75
Monday	676	112	16.57
Tuesday	418	77	18.42
Wednesday	478	79	16.53
Thursday	549	96	17.49
Friday	732	133	18.17
Saturday	855	136	15.91

Saturday winners
from major courses
next time out.

Day	Bets	Wins	Win%
Sunday	149	31	20.81
Monday	103	26	25.24
Tuesday	156	26	16.67
Wednesday	258	64	24.81
Thursday	289	65	22.49
Friday	521	97	18.62
Saturday	1098	195	17.76

The opposite table shows winners on Major courses that win on a Saturday the next time they run on a Monday win 25.24% of the time. If they return on a Saturday, they only win 17.76% of the time. a difference of 7.5%. You will always see this pattern, this data is well worth considering when making your selections.

Day of the Week

The Table below shows Horses that have won on a Monday the next time they run over a Fifteen-year period. The table shows that Monday winners only win on a Saturday next time out 14.7% of the time. Compared to winning on a Monday 17.68% of the time. It is obvious that the better races with more prize money are run on a Saturday, but the statistics are well worth considering.

Criteria	Bets	Wins	Win%
Sunday	507	75	14.7
Monday	1182	209	17.68
Tuesday	895	153	17.1
Wednesday	1010	164	16.24
Thursday	1108	185	16.7
Friday	1400	234	16.71
Saturday	1946	287	14.75

As a further demonstration of how important the day of the week is the table below shows favourites over the last 5 years.

Favourites over the last 5 years

Criteria	Win%	Place%
Sunday	32.27	58.7
Monday	33.51	61.73
Tuesday	32.55	59.83
Wednesday	32.47	60.41
Thursday	34.26	61.43
Friday	31.31	58.47
Saturday	31.52	57.42

Day of the Week

The table shows that favourites win on a Monday 2% more often than they do on a Saturday. This shows that races on a Monday are easier to predict.

The table below shows all horses that won on a Saturday next time out over a ten-year period from all courses.

Saturday winners next time out. All courses

Criteria	Win%	Place%
Sunday	15.18	35.22
Monday	20.77	42.83
Tuesday	17.49	39.16
Wednesday	17.81	38
Thursday	17.36	39.49
Friday	16.62	39.06
Saturday	15	34.54

This demonstrates that horses that win on a Saturday. The next time they run they win on a Monday 20.77% of the time. But only win again on a Saturday 15% of the time. The difference is very nearly 6%. Again, this demonstrates that races run on a Monday are easier to win than any other day of the week. This book does not cover National Hunt racing in the same detail but the difference there is 10%.

Day of the Week

The big differences in the two days are in Non Handicaps. The table below shows that horses that win on a Monday when returning next time out on the days of the week shown. The table is over a Fifteen-year period. Should they return on Monday they have a 25.69%-win rate. Should they return on a Saturday the win rate is down to 13.19% a difference of 12%. In the place Market returning on a Monday, they place 48.62% of the time but only place on a Saturday 33.63% of the time.

Criteria	Bets	Wins	Win%	Place%
Sunday	77	16	20.78	49.35
Monday	109	28	25.69	48.62
Tuesday	124	19	15.32	33.06
Wednesday	181	33	18.23	35.91
Thursday	222	37	16.67	37.84
Friday	280	49	17.5	36.07
Saturday	455	60	13.19	33.63

Though the amount of data here is quite small it does show a trend. It may or may not be something that helps you to decide on a selection.

This next section I could have put in the favourites chapter or the Chapter for trainers. As a demonstration for the importance of the day of the week I thought this would be a better place for it.

The table on the following page shows the performance of two trainers John Gosden and W J Haggas. Both trainers at the top of their game. The data has been taken over the last 10 years. Between them they have fewer runners on a Sunday, Monday, and Tuesday than any other day. On a Monday or a Tuesday if any of the two trainers have a horse that starts as the favourite, they have over 50% success rate.

Day of The Week

Whereas on a Saturday their runners that start favourite only win 33.5% of the time. The Monday/Tuesday favourites show a profit at SP as well as on the exchanges. Whereas the Thursday/Friday/Saturday favourites show a considerable loss.

Between them they had a maximum losing run of seven just once and a winning run of eight twice. They had a place losing run of four just once and a winning place run of seventeen once.

Criteria	Bets	Wins	Win%	P/L(SP)	P/L(BF)
Sunday	155	63	40.65	-23.8	-19.53
Monday	221	114	51.58	18.17	28
Tuesday	211	107	50.71	33.46	46.09
Wednesday	344	137	39.83	-6.26	11.19
Thursday	405	157	38.77	-52.97	-39.5
Friday	633	240	37.91	-55.33	-30.89
Saturday	827	277	33.49	-80.85	-48.79

You need to bear in mind that 50% winners mean 50% losers too. You still need to do your homework on their runners. There are other trainers that make considerably more profit on these days but with a smaller win %, for example R A Fahay on Monday/Tuesday results below.

Criteria	Bets	Wins	Win%	P/L(SP)	P/L(BF)
Monday	186	69	37.1	29.68	40.28
Tuesday	144	58	40.28	24.44	34

Day Of The Week

One thing you may want to check is HRB ratings, providing they are rated in the top 6 in the ratings table they make a profit at SP, outside the top 6 they make as slight loss at SP, with the top rated winning 58.54% of the time.

The table below shows horses that won last time out how they perform when they reappear on each day of the week.

Criteria	Bets	Wins	Win%
Sunday	4267	733	17.18
Monday	6438	1159	18
Tuesday	6143	1102	17.94
Wednesday	1384	1384	16.7
Thursday	9653	1713	17.75
Friday	13439	2290	17.04
Saturday	20849	3090	14.82

This just goes to show that it is easier to win on Monday's than any other day of the week to be more precise the quality of the races makes Monday slightly easier. There is 4% difference between reappearing on a Monday to reappearing on a Saturday. The percentages are the same for horses that finished second last time out. they win on Monday 19.65% of the time, but races run on a Saturday for horses that finished second last time out win only 15.62% of the time. It does not matter which day they won on last time out the results are about the same no matter what day they won on. It is the day they run on next time out that makes a difference.

Place Betting

Betting For Place Only

I am always surprised that betting for a place is as controversial as it appears to be. I hear arguments for and against and could agree with both sides. I can understand that some would get a positive feeling about getting a more constant return. I also understand that some would think the value is not there.

Going back in time when I thought I knew it all and had this backing horses' game sussed. I am talking of about 45+ years ago I remember backing 16 straight losers at a range of prices. The thing about every single one of them was that they all placed. I thought I would start backing Each Way the next four all finished fourth. but that is just the way it goes sometimes. I remember thinking at the time if only I could just back for a place, obviously this was before the days of the Exchanges.

These days we are blessed with a multiple of choices. With the addition of the exchange's bookmakers have had to become far more competitive than they used to be. The place backer has so much information at his fingertips that with care it is possible to make a profit by place only. The only times I ever back for place on the Exchanges is when I have a selection between 4/1 and around 6/1 and there is another runner or even two runners that I am not quite sure about. I occasionally would make sure I cover my win stake plus some for a small profit. That is providing the place price is greater than 25% of the win price.

Would I back a favourite for a place? Extremely rarely and I can tell you why that is very easily. The table on the following page shows how often Favourites win and how often they place. The data has been taken over a Ten-year period with races on the flat in the UK in races with 8-15 runners. Irelands figures come up slightly differently which we will also cover. The other table is for the 3rd favourite in races with 8-15 runners.

Betting For Place Only

Favourites UK

Criteria	Bets	Win%	Place%	Finish 2nd/3rd%
Non Hcp	7600	36.59	70.55	33.96
Handicaps	17001	25.42	56.06	30.64

3rd Favourite UK

Criteria	Bets	Win%	Place%	Finish 2nd/3rd%
Non Hcp	7185	12.78	45.21	32.43
Handicaps	15496	13.15	38.96	25.81

Looking at the favourites table first you can see that the favourite in non-handicap races win more often than they place either second or third. In Handicap races there is only 5% difference it would seem to me a waste to neglect the win in favour of the place.

The third Favourite places either second or third as often as the Favourite wins. The average place price for the third Favourite is 2.3 in non-handicaps and 2.54 In Handicaps both above even money. However, that alone does not make backing the 3rd 4th or 5th favourite for a place profitable you would lose money on Betfair, particularly if you are paying 5% commission.

You would need to find a way of eliminating a great deal of the horses that do not place. HRB provides you with so much data for you to be able to do just that it is a case of experimentation to see what works.

Betting For Place Only

Irish percentage figures are below

Favourite 8-15 runners

Criteria	Bets	Win%	Place%	2nd/3rd%
Non Hcp	3112	36.12	70.15	34.03
Handicaps	3181	22.48	51.62	29.14

3rd Favourites 8-15 Runners

Criteria	Bets	Win%	Place%	2nd/3rd%
Non Hcp	2924	12.93	45.04	32.11
Handicaps	2896	12.22	37.61	25.39

The main difference is that in Ireland the Favourite does not win or place as often as they do in the UK. The difference is so slight it is negligible really, we still have the percentage figures. In as much that the third Favourite places either second or third as often as the favourite wins.

I suppose I can see the sense in backing anything bar the favourite for a place unless the Favourite was 4/1 or above, I would not really be interested in backing for a place. That is just me it is each to their own.

As I have said you need to find a way of eliminating losing bets if you are looking at system betting. You could start by looking at trainers whose horses place on a regular basis based on past information. A table showing the results of that is on the following page. These are trainers whose horses have started as 3rd favourite and shown a profit over the ten-year period.

Betting For Place Only

Results of Profitable trainers of 3rd favourites

Criteria	Bets	Win%	Place%	2nd/3rd%
Non Hcp	1427	13.81	51.23	37.42
Handicaps	4212	15.38	45.89	30.51

The results are quite favourable with higher percentages of placed horses ending up with a nice profit if you backed them all for a place which is highly unlikely. As the markets are live it is difficult to say which horse will end up as the third Favourite.

On top of that this is taken from ten years of historical data. Which has no bearing on what will happen now or in the future.

The majority of people do not have the time to sit and watch every race just to see which horse is going to end up third or fourth favourite. The solution maybe to take the forecast 3rd Favourite as the results are similar if not slightly better. Of course, you will not know if your selection will end up as Favourite or 10th Favourite but as the results are virtually as good maybe it does not matter. The table on the following page shows the percentages of the forecast 3rd favourite in both Handicap and non-handicap races. Just for comparison I have copied the table of the Starting Price 3rd favourite below it.

The reason for the difference in races run is that for the forecast favourite I have eliminated races where there are joint third favourites. You can see that the forecast third favourites win slightly more often but place slightly less often the differences are quite minor really.

Betting For Place Only

Percentages of the Forecast 3rd Favourite

Criteria	Bets	Win%	Place%
Non Hcp	6018	13.51	43.55
Handicaps	11070	13.36	38.29

Percentages of the Starting Price 3rd Favourite

Criteria	Bets	Win%	Place%
Non Hcp	7185	12.78	45.21
Handicaps	15496	13.15	38.96

All Weather Percentages of the Forecast Price 3rd Favourite

Criteria	Bets	Win%	Place%
Non Hcp	3764	14.19	48.14
Handicaps	9845	13.45	38.67

The third table is for the forecast price of the third favourite on the All Weather you can see that they compare very favourably with both sets of figures above. You still need to do some extra weeding out of qualifiers though even on the All Weather as you will not make a profit overall. There seems to be more drift in the market on the All Weather some drift out to 16/1 and 20/1 with higher prices on the Exchanges. Following trainers that have a High Profit/Loss on the All Weather in the place market could be worth looking at.

Betting For Place Only

Another angle you may want to look at is only having selections on courses where the going has been assessed to be either Good, Good to Firm or Firm. The 3rd Favourite places on going assessed as either Heavy or Good to Soft less than 40% of the time whereas on Firm ground, they place almost 45% of the time.

Strangely the best races for the 3rd Favourite to place in are.
Sellers 46.52%
Maidens 46.91%
Novices 48.37%
Handicap Claimers 53.85%
Handicap Sellers 48.35%
Handicap Maidens 46.58%

Just sticking to those events which are the type of races most professionals would leave well alone would massively reduce the number of selections. It would also increase your win rate. If you then used that coupled with one or more other suggestions, you could have the basis of a decent system.

You may also want to consider the SP of the 3rd Favourite as the place percentage starts to drop off considerably after the price reaches 6/1.

Though I have been evaluating the 3rd Favourite throughout this chapter you can of course use the 2nd Favourite or the 4th or 5th, you just need to do your homework on the data.

Betting For Place Only

If you are confident about your selections, you may want to look at backing the Favourite to win and third Favourite to place. Making sure you cover your win bet with the place bet should the favourite get beaten. You do however need a high success rate to make this work the best scenario is that the favourite wins and the third favourite places. The other side of this is that the Favourite does not win, and the third favourite does not place. Like everything else in this game, you need a high success rate.

Another angle could be to only have a selection at tracks that show a high percentage of both Favourites winning and/or third Favourites placing for example at Ascot only 34.43% of third favourites have placed in the first 3. Whereas at Beverley 45.94% of third Favourites have placed in the first three.

Another angle could be to play the percentages and only bet in races with five runners to get the third Favourite in the 1st two which in theory is a 40% chance. Or races with eight runners to get your selection in the first three which in theory is a 37.5% chance.

There are thousands of angles you could look at by manipulating the data within Horseracebace. For every single position in both the forecast market and at Starting Price. I find deleting runners with certain types of headgear helps in some types of races you will find Fillies do not fair very well depending on how many Colts and Geldings there are in the field. This is something that I have noticed over the years at the courses particularly the courses with stiff finishes.

If place betting is your thing because of the more constant profitable returns, then fill your boots with manipulating data to find a favourable position. Before you start to invest though run your system for a few months, Horseracebase lets you see the results from the saved date of your system that is an excellent pointer to see if your system will work in the long term.

Betting For Place Only

One area that you may want to look at is backing for a place in Non handicap races with between 6-7 runners where Betfair are paying three places. If you back the outsider of the field for a place. over the last seven years you would have made £3400 to a £20 stake.

However, you will need a substantial bank to achieve this as it once went fifty-eight races without an outsider placing. With a place percentage of just 17%, that would not be unusual. You can of course back the favourite and the outsider for a place with the same stake. This would give you virtually the same profit but with a strike rate of 40.59% that is far more palatable. It just means that while you are waiting for your outsiders to place your favourite bet is saving you some of the stake on the outsider. In the calculations I have also removed horses wearing blinkers or a hood as these always seem to lose money.

Unfortunately the situation is not the same in Ireland. Irish racing needs different set of data to make a profit. In fact, following the same data in Ireland it pays to lay the outsider of 6-7 runners for a place. not a strategy I would recommend as it would mean laying at prices above 100/1 in some cases.

Horseracebase provides you with tens of thousands of diverse ways to analyse data. I have only touched on a fraction of what could be achieved here.

The Going

The Going

I have to say that I do not take too much notice of the going when assessing the form of a horse. I know of one trainer that insists that the going is everything, one of the biggest excuses that a jockey gives for horses not performing is "The Going" he/she did not act on The Going, if it was softer, if it was firmer if there was no going at all.

I know of one quite famous owner who once said "he could write a book about the number of excuses a Jockey/Trainer gives for a horse getting beaten," Going to Soft, Too hard, Grass too Long, Too Short, Too Green, Not Green enough, Frightened by a Bird, It was raining, Distracted by the crowd, race too soon after last race, Not soon enough, you name it and the excuse would have been given.

Having said that I do not pay too much attention to the going there is data that suggests it does have some effect. The table below shows horses that placed previously on Good or Firm going compared to those that placed on Heavy or Soft to Heavy last time they ran. **Going This time   Going Last Time**

Going this time	Good or Firm	Heavy
Heavy	26%	23.9%
Soft To Heavy	27.5%	23.04%
Soft	26.29%	24.56%
Yeilding To Soft	28.18%	22.66%
Yeilding	28.31%	24.64%
Good To Yeilding	27.46%	30.07%
Good To Soft	25.49%	23.62%
Good	25.92%	24.32%
Good To Firm	28.22%	24.62%
Firm	32.03	20%

The Going

The table clearly shows that horses that placed last time out on Good to Firm ground fare better in their following race than horses that placed on Heavy or Soft to Heavy ground. The percentages are taken from the first two in the market next time out.

Though the percentages may be small there is still a difference and taking form from races on Heavy ground particularly. May not be as dependable as that taken from ground classed as Good to Firm this may point you towards some false favourites.

The table below really shows there is a Going advantage it shows that if a horse won on Heavy ground, it is likely to win 3% more often when returning on Heavy Ground than a horse that won on Good Ground. It is the same when they both encounter Soft Going on Good to Soft, they fair about the same. As the ground gets firmer is where winners on Good Ground really come into their own and Heavy Ground winners start to struggle the data is taken over a twenty-year period.

Criteria for their following race	Won on Heavy last time	Won on Good Last time
Heavy	17.55	14.69
Soft	20	16.43
Good To Soft	17.27	17.07
Good	11.63	17.21
Good To Firm	11.11	16.97
Firm	11.76	22.08

The Going

The table below shows how favourites fair on different types of going. You can see that the firmer the going the more dependable the form. Just for comparison the second table shows how the fourth favourites fare, they win more times on Heavy than they do on Good Going

How Favourites fare on different types of going.

Criteria	Win%
Heavy	28.92
Soft	30.35
Good To Soft	29.47
Good	29.91
Good To Firm	32.6
Firm	34.25

How the Fourth Favourites fare on different types of going.

Criteria	Win%
Heavy	11.13
Soft	10.2
Good To Soft	9.38
Good	9.94
Good To Firm	9.98
Firm	10.2

Trading

Trading

I do not trade on horses or in any other betting market I am far more interested in the racing itself and looking for winners through statistics and form. I am particularly interested in being at the course to get the most pleasure from Horse Racing.

There are endless videos on Youtube about trading some I watch with interest just to see how the market fluctuates on the exchanges it does not fluctuate anywhere near as rapidly on course. There is one trader I can whole heartedly recommend that if you are interested in trading, you should listen too. He is knowledgeable on the subject in a diverse number of markets. He makes very interesting Youtube videos that are also entertaining as well as informative. Caan Berry is a professional Trader check his videos if that is where your interest lies.

Now having said that I do of course know a number of people who like to dabble in trading part time but would really like to make it full time. There are certain things in racing that would favour a trader such as.

- Which trainer's horses are likely to drift in the market under what circumstances.
- Under what circumstances are favourites likely to get turned over in running.
- What type of races are the forecast favourites likely to be false favourites and are likely to drift in the live market.
- How can we recognise a horse that is not value for money very early on and is likely to shorten in the market.

Trading

Let us take a look at the first point.

- Which trainers horses are likely to drift in the market under what circumstances.

This is an easy one to answer the majority of drifting horses are in Handicap races. Bookmakers never want to take a risk on horses from top stables. They always forecast them at quite low prices then wait to see where the money is coming in from. You can run a list of all horses that were the forecast favourite then ended up being 4th favourite or greater. If you then check which training yard they come from it will always be the top yards. The majority of drifters come in Class 3,4 and 5 races with Class 4 and 5 being the biggest culprits. Whether these horses end up winning or not at this point is immaterial. The facts are they were forecast as being favourite early when the bookmakers open their books. By the time the race comes around they have drifted to fourth favourite or even lower. This is the time when the trader needs to get out as a new picture is about to begin once the race is under way. If the horse is from a top yard and finished in the first three in a class 5 race last time out and this time it is running in a class 3 or Class 4 race there is very high chance it will drift in the market. Another way of looking at this is that the horses that last ran in a class 5 race Handicap and are now entered in class 3 or 4 race, and they stay as favourite and do not drift 34.22% win. Which is a high percentage in Handicaps. Anything placing or just running in a class 5 or class 6 race now that is the forecast favourite in class 3 or 4 providing it did not win either Comfortably or Easily has a very good chance of drifting in the market.

The reverse of this is that if the forecast favourite is from a small yard and top yards have runners in the race then that is also highly likely to drift in the market particularly if it is in a higher-class race.

Trading

Now let us take a look at the second point

- Under what circumstances are favourites likely to get turned over in running.

The first point to look at is the going the table below shows all favourites in all races over a fifteen-year period how they faired on the different types of going.

Criteria	Bets	Wins	Win%
Heavy	1671	487	29.14
Soft	8206	2511	30.06
Good to Soft	9483	2838	29.93
Good	18763	5694	30.35
Good to Firm	22725	7524	33.11
Firm	1441	523	36.29

It is obvious that favourites fare better on Good to Firm and Firm Going than they do on anything softer than Good. In the case of Heavy to Firm there is a 7% difference. You may think that it is Handicap races that are the biggest provider of the difference. In fact, it is the non-handicaps where the biggest differences come in.

Non Handicap table

Criteria	Bets	Wins	Win%
Heavy	539	179	33.21
Soft	2755	1071	38.87
Good to Soft	3218	1227	38.13
Good	6448	2414	37.44
Good to Firm	7719	3164	40.99
Firm	360	182	50.56

Trading

Though the data is small between Heavy and Firm there is a 17% difference with a 7.7% difference between Heavy and Good to Firm. I suppose what you could take away from this is the fact that even in non-handicaps where the price is likely to be very short the favourite will get turned over more often than it will prevail.

We can keep breaking these details down even further. The difference between Male and Females is also quite pronounced. The tables below are the differences between Males and Female favourites on the different types of going in non-handicaps.

	Criteria	Bets	Wins	Win%
	Heavy	368	117	31.79
	Soft	1802	676	37.51
	Good to Soft	2168	820	37.82
Males	Good	4216	1640	38.9
	Good to Firm	4921	2084	42.35
	Firm	194	103	53.09

	Criteria	Bets	Wins	Win%
	Heavy	171	62	36.26
	Soft	953	395	41.45
Females	Good to Soft	1050	407	38.76
	Good	2232	774	34.68
	Good to Firm	2798	1080	38.6
	Firm	166	79	47.59

The difference between Heavy and Firm for Females is 10% whereas for Males it is 21%.

Trading

We can go on breaking these figures down in so many ways it would fill a whole book. For traders it is worth doing just that, the next thing I would do is look at the different courses. Particularly those with uphill finishes also I would look at where the favourite was in the weight scale too. Looking at the area in this book on courses and that on trainers could also give the trader some advantage. If I were into trading in a big way that is exactly what I would do to try and gain some advantage over other traders.

The next point was.

- What type of races are the forecast favourites likely to be false favourites and are likely to drift in the live market.

This has been partly covered by the first point however there are other ways to look at this. The track where the Forecast Favourite drifts the most before start time is Windsor.

Almost every Monday night in one race or another a forecast favourite drifts beyond the first three in the market. I have given some examples of recent drifters below, Horseracebase gives you all these details for every horse.

> 04/09/23 Tiors f/c 5/2f odds Sp 5/1
> 04/09/23 Fullforward f/c 7/2f odds SP 9/1
> 26/08/23 One Step Beyond f/c 2/1f odds SP 13/2
> 17/8/23 Crimson Angel f/c 9/2f odds Sp 14/1

All the above won their previous race and were up in class in one way or another. Horseracebase gives you the following information for every horse and every race.

FC=Forecast, PLS=Pre Live Show, LVS=Live Show, SP=Starting Price.

Race, Pos,FC, PLSOpen, PLSMin, PLSMax, LVSOpen, LVSMin, LVSMax, SP

Trading

A table that HRB produces for each horse is shown below.

FC=Forecast, PLS=Pre Live Show, LVS=Live Show, SP=Starting Price.

Race	Pos	FC	PLS Open	PLS Min	PLS Max	LVS Open	LVS Min	LVS Max	SP
25.08.2022 Carlisle	4th	11/2	7/2	7/2	6/1	11/2	11/2	6/1	6/1
1.08.2022 Ayr	1st	3/1	2/1	2/1	11/4	5/2	5/2	3/1	3/1
11.07.2022 Ayr	1st	16/1	25/1	18/1	25/1	22/1	22/1	40/1	40/1
18.06.2022 Perth	PU	100/1	80/1	80/1	100/1	100/1	80/1	150/1	150/1
9.06.2022 Uttoxeter	11th	50/1	100/1	100/1	100/1	100/1	100/1	125/1	125/1
3.11.2021 Musselburgh	PU	50/1	28/1	14/1	28/1	18/1	18/1	50/1	50/1
12.03.2021 Dundalk	3rd	10/1	15/2	7/1	11/1	9/1	9/1	10/1	10/1
1.02.2021 Dundalk	3rd	10/1	4/1	4/1	5/1	4/1	4/1	4/1	4/1
15.01.2021 Dundalk	8th	12/1	16/1	9/1	16/1	9/1	17/2	10/1	17/2
23.11.2020 Dundalk	7th	50/1	66/1	66/1	100/1	100/1	100/1	150/1	150/1
17.09.2020 Naas	12th	20/1	20/1	20/1	22/1	22/1	22/1	33/1	25/1

You could not wish for more information than that provided in your search for horses that are likely to drift. Your homework will be very worthwhile.

The next point we asked was.

- How can we recognise a horse that is not value for money early on and is likely to shorten in the market.

It is difficult to say what drives a shortening price when I list out the trainers whose horses have shortened in the market the same culprits are there it is all the top trainers once again. The shortening price does not mean they are any more likely to win as the data does not bear that out. It does not look like it is stable confidence when it comes to the leading trainers. It is more likely to be either punter confidence or bookmakers fear. The data is all there in HRB to be investigated.

Trading

I have listed in the table on the following page trainers whose horses opened as favourites but drifted to beyond third favourite. It is worth taking note of these trainers whose horses drift in the market and then do not go on to win. This could be an angle you may be able to exploit.

Trading

Criteria	Bets	Wins	Win%
Easterby, T D	119	11	9.24
OMeara, D	170	19	11.18
Dods, M	72	6	8.33
Burke, K R	45	3	6.67
Hannon (Jnr), Richard	94	11	11.7
Ellison, B	31	1	3.23
Weld, D K	61	5	8.2
Hills, Charles	39	3	7.69
Suroor, Saeed Bin	26	1	3.85
Quinn, J J	59	7	11.86
Easterby, M W	54	6	11.11
Williams, S C	45	4	8.89
Walker, Ed	39	4	10.26
Dunlop, E A L	44	4	9.09
Prescott, Sir Mark	30	3	10
Carr, Mrs R A	59	7	11.86
Charlton, Roger/Harry	27	2	7.41
Cox, C G	38	3	7.89
Palmer, Hugo	26	2	7.69
Smart, B	18	1	5.56
Murtagh, J P	29	2	6.9
Mullins, W P	14	0	0
Hughes, Richard	34	4	11.76
Guest, R C	19	1	5.26
Perratt, Miss L A	13	0	0
Alston, E J	13	0	0

Analysing Data

Analysing Data

Throughout this book I have tried to stick to data that can be relied upon. Like data on the Going, Colt and Fillies, trainer's percentages etc. It is easy to show data from given years or from trainer's horses or even Jockeys that cannot be relied upon for future events. I will demonstrate what I mean with the table below.

This table shows trainers that have made a consistent profit every year in the place market. I have taken all trainers that had a place return greater than 25% in the place market that made a profit in the last 7 years.

	Bets	Plc%(BF)	P/L(Plc)
All	18989	31.31	2217.7
2023	2661	30.51	153.02
2022	3219	32.15	892.33
2021	3143	31.63	269.76
2020	2515	31.98	218.23
2019	2460	30.85	340.73
2018	2476	31.54	216.78
2017	2515	30.22	126.85

Wow we are in here a profit every year to a £1.00 stake let us lump on. No STOP, when you have data like this over however many years you care to name. Test it over further years or miss two years out get your results. When you have done that then add those two years back in. Let us add another three years to our data above.

Result at the top of the following page.

Analysing Data

	Bets	Plc%(BF)	P/L(Plc)
All	25467	30.9	1909.99
2023	2661	30.51	153.02
2022	3219	32.15	892.33
2021	3143	31.63	269.76
2020	2515	31.98	218.23
2019	2460	30.85	340.73
2018	2476	31.54	216.78
2017	2515	30.22	126.85
2016	2371	30.03	-52.77
2015	2142	28.94	-186.71
2014	1965	30.13	-68.23

The three years we just added all lost money using the same data. If I add in another three years, they will also lose money. This is because I have made the data fit the results. I like to look for information as well as data information on courses, trainers etc, Ratings and Speed Ratings are positive results that can be relied upon to a point. They are not in the same class as analysing data.

You can of course come up with some excellent systems using past data. All I am saying is double check it before laying out any money. HRB shows your results of your system by last seven days, last fourteen, days and so on, the most useful one is (Performance since saved date) it is worth waiting several months to see if your system is working.

The Betting Shop punter

We have talked about Ratings, Speed Ratings, Trainers, Courses and all sorts of things that if you had the data, you could look at finding a way to carve yourself a niche. There are a number of different companies that provide data, and you could use others in a similar way. What happens if you do not have access to a large data base like Horseracebase. You only have the Racing Post hanging on the wall at your local bookmakers. How then do you sort the Wheat from the Chaff?

I do classify courses when looking for something that may have better form than appears at face value. My classifications of courses looking at Class 1 or 2 races are listed below.

Groups if you are assessing races that are
either Group or Class 1 or 2 on the flat.

Group 1	Group2	Group 3
Newmarket Ascot Salisbury Newbury Sandown	Epsom Brighton Doncaster York Haydock Nottingham Bath Leicester Kempton Goodwood Windsor Wetherby Hamilton Chester Ripon	Ayr Chelmsford City Thirsk Yarmouth Newcastle Pontefract Southwell Wolverhampton Redcar Ffos Las Beverley Catterick Lingfield Musselburgh Carlisle Chepstow Warwick

Groups if you are assessing a
Class 3 or 4 race on the flat.

Group 1	Group 2	Group 3
Newbury Newmarket Haydock York Salisbury Wetherby Ascot Sandown Goodwood	Yarmouth Nottingham Doncaster Thirsk Chester Leicester Windsor Bath Epsom Ffos Las Carlisle Kempton Hamilton Pontefract Musselburgh Beverley Chelmsford City Ripon Catterick Ayr	Brighton Newcastle Lingfield Chepstow Redcar Warwick Wolverhampton Southwell

As well as being grouped into these three categories they are
also in order of importance in each Group. When assessing
Class 3 and 4 races the All-Weather courses are about on a
par with Brighton, Chepstow, and Redcar.

My Classification of courses when assessing races
in Class 5,6 and 7 on the flat.

Group1	Group 2	Group 3	Group 4
		Ayr	
		Bath	
	Sandown	Pontefract	
	Haydock	Epsom	
	Goodwood	Ripon	
	Nottingham	Chester	
Ascot	Windsor	Carlisle	Lingfield
Newmarket	Doncaster	Chepstow	Newcastle
York	Warwick	Redcar	Wolverhampton
Newbury	Salisbury	Chelmsford City	Southwell
	Folkestone	Thirsk	
	Wetherby	Hamilton	
	Yarmouth	Catterick	
	Ffos Las	Brighton	
	Leicester	Musselburgh	
		Kempton	
		Beverley	

As well as being grouped into these three categories they are
also in order of importance in each Group, the four All
Weather Courses are in group four as they produce the fewest
winners in the classes being assessed on the flat, more about
the All Weather grouping later.

Grouping Courses like this is just an aid you will also need to consider distance beaten. I have based my groups on horses either winning or at least being within four lengths of the winner. Anything greater than four lengths you need to start moving down the hierarchy of the group or down to the next group down. The value of the race may also be criteria you may want to consider.

One of the best ways to use course groups or the hierarchy of courses is in non-handicaps. I will use an example from Newcastle 02/11/2023 Class 5 £3500 eleven runners.

The reason I would pick this race is because there are only four runners that have had a previous race two of those are 200/1 plus. We can discount both of those. John Gosden has a runner, John's runners at Newcastle need to be respected however she is 20/1 which would mean there is little confidence behind her. Simon Crisford has a runner though recently his newcomers have been taking a race or two to get fully wound up even when starting at short prices Simon's runner today Rose Applause was forecast at 8/1, opened at 4/1 after touching 6/4 drifted to 3/1.

The two runners with experience are at the top of the market Lou Lous Gift 13/8 and Staincliff 3/1. Lou Lous Gift last race was at Yarmouth a Class 4 £5K race. Staincliffs Last Race was at Sandown Class 4 £5K race. I have set them out in a simple table below.

Horse	Course	Class	Value	Btn By
Lou Lous Gift	Yarmouth	4	£5K	5.3L
Staincliff	Sandown	4	£5K	1L

Both horses ran on a Group 2 course last time out Sandown is the top of the Group 2 courses and Yarmouth is third from bottom. If you also consider, the distance beaten there is only one choice to run with.

1st: Staincliff 3/1.
2nd: Lou Lous Gift 13/8f.
3rd: Rosa Applause 3/1.

This was a quite easy race to assess the Betting Shop Punter is probably not in there to look for one race though they may well be better off if they were. Therefore, let us look at another race run at Bath a Class 4 £10K race the first four in the betting are listed below.

Horse	Course	Class	Value	Group/ Position	Btn By	SP
Hot Fuss	Haydock	Listed	23K	1/3	5.9L	5/4
Calvert	Bath	4	11K	2/8	6L	11/2
Dallas Star	Newmarket	3	8K	1/2	4.5L	11/2
Palace Green	Newbury	2	16K	1/1	UR	7/1

Palace Green has the highest credentials however we have no idea how good he is. he unseated his rider on his only outing starting price is 7/1 must have a big chance. As Calvert 11/2 is the only one that last ran on a Group 2 course and was beaten 6 Lengths, we can discount him. Dallas Star 11/2 Ran at Newmarket, 2nd in the list only beaten 4.5L. Hot Fuss 5/4f Ran in a Listed race beaten by 5.9L. I would not be interested in Hot Fuss at 5/4, but with Dallas Star and Calvert both being 11/2. We have discounted Calvert, to me that makes Dallas Star an Excellent Each Way bet.

The Betting Shop Punter

The Result of the race is

1st Dallas Star 11/2

2nd Hot Fuss 5/4(fav)

3rd: Palace Green 7/1

4th Calvert 11/2

Not the easiest of races to work out but we were getting value E/W about Dallas Star. I looked at it as an extremely good chance with a big likely hood of getting our money back or a winner as it turned out Dallas Star won at 11/2.

As I have pointed out it is better to use the grouping of the tracks in non-handicaps let us see how it works out in a Handicap Nursery on the same day at Bath.

Horse	Course	Class	Value	Group/Position	Btn By
Whoop Whoop	Ffos Las	5	4K	2/12	3.5L
Goodeveningmrbond (IRE)	Haydock	5	5K	2/2	7.5L
Whiteley Way	Lingfield	5	4K	4/1	2L
Newport Bay (IRE)	Catterick	5	5K	3/13	3L
Crooked Crown	Ffos Las	5	4K	2/12	6L
Nelson Rose	Kempton	5	4K	3/16	4.4L
Black Jack Davey	Kempton	6	3K	3/16	7.9L
Kiss And Run	Windsor	5	4K	2/5	4L

The table above shows every runner and where they ran last time out, the class of race, the value of the race, which Group it is in from our table on page 192 and how far they were beaten by.

The one you would eliminate straight away is Black Jack Davey, being the only horse that ran in a Class 6 race for 3K and beaten by nearly 8 Lengths. The next two I would eliminate is Goodeveningmrbond and Crooked Crown as they were beaten 7.5L.

and 6 Lengths. The tables are made up from horses that have
finished within 4 Lengths of the winner. In the case of
Goodeveneingmrbond we would have to drop him to the bottom of
his group 2 at least. Whiteley Way ran at Lingfield top of group 4
only beaten by 2 Lengths; I would not write her off just yet.
Newport Bay ran at Catterick 13th in the group 3 table Beaten by 3
Lengths. That would automatically rub Nelson Rose out as she was
beaten by 4.4 Lengths on a course 16th in Group 3. Whoop Whoop
who started favourite ran at Ffos Lass 12th in the table in Group 2,
Beaten by 3.5 Lengths. That leaves us with Kiss and Run who ran
at Windsor 5th in the table of Group 2 beaten by just 4 Lengths.
No reduction for Kiss and Run. the result of the race is below.

1st: Kiss and Run 20/1
2nd Whiteley Way 11/2
3rd Black Jack Davy 9/1
4th Nelson Rose 13/2
5th Whoop Whoop 7/2 (Fav)
6th Goodeveneningmrbond 4/1
7th Crooked Crown 7/1
8th Newport Bay 5/1

This is a race on the same card as Staincliff our earlier 3/1 winner. I
appreciate that you cannot stand in the bookies writing all this out,
but you get the picture. You do have to bear in mind that courses
like Epsom 4th in the table of group 3 when it comes to Epsom
Derby time it elevates the course to Group 1 standard that is why
when looking at Class 1 and 2 races Epsom is the top of the table in
Group 2.
Many Handicap races that you could analyse will not work out as
simple as Kiss And Run's race. The form will be mixed the distance
beaten by will overlap with the groupings. Horses will come out of
the blue to run a race they have never been able too before it is part
of the fun of the sport.

I do not want to sound like a broken record, but I do need to keep pointing out that course classification is an aid to finding fair value selections. It should be used with other methods where you need to make decisions as to when and where to invest. I can give an example below.

I can show just two horses from a Race at Newmarket

Horse	Course	Class	Value	Group/ Position	Won By
Beautiful Love (IRE)	Newmarket	4	4K	1/1	+1L
Regal Jubilee	Windsor	5	4K	2/11	+7L

Here you have two horses both won their last race one at Newmarket who is top of Group one for listed races and the other 11th in Group 2. You may automatically select the horse that won at Newmarket and started the 5/2 JFav. However, the Windsor winner Regal Jubilee won very easily by 7 Lengths you therefore must assume that she is capable of far better.

Regal Jubilee won the race at 9/1 Beautiful Love was 4th.

The horse that finished 3rd at 14/1 also previously won its last race comfortably at Redcar.

If you cannot decide between two or three horses then leave the race alone there will be better selections that come along.

The Betting Shop Punter

For Irish racing, the Hierarchy of courses that produce winners is shown below. I take winners or horses that finish within 3 lengths of the winner. as the percentages drop off markedly when beaten by distances greater than three lengths.

Irish Courses past 13 years	Irish Courses past 20 years
Leopardstown	Curragh
Galway	Leopardstown
Curragh	Galway
Tipperary	Punchestown
Naas	Naas
Punchestown	Tipperary
Wexford	Navan
Listowel	Limerick
Navan	Wexford
Laytown	Gowran Park
Gowran Park	Listowel
Down Royal	Down Royal
Limerick	Fairyhouse
Cork	Laytown
Fairyhouse	Dundalk
Dundalk	Cork
Downpatrick	Downpatrick
Killarney	Killarney
Ballinrobe	Roscommon
Bellewstown	Bellewstown
Roscommon	Ballinrobe
Sligo	Sligo
Clonmel	Tramore
Tramore	Clonmel
Kilbeggan	Tralee
Thurles	Kilbeggan
	Thurles

I have printed two tables for Irish Racing the one I use is for the last 13 years I have listed another table for the past 20 Years as there has been a slight change in the percentages. Particularly over the last 10 years. If you prefer to have more Data under your belt, then use the 20-year table.

Ironically the only course to show a level stake profit over both 13 and 20 years are horses that last ran at Laytown. I believe that is because people do not give Laytown the credit it deserves. Laytown is another course that I have not visited in Ireland. I am very much looking forward to being there on the beach in the next couple of years. Let us look at race run at Dundalk 3rd November 2023, a £5500 race over 5F. Most of the runners either ran at Dundalk last time out or at Navan and were all beaten by greater than 3 Lengths, including Sams Express the 7/2 Fav who was beaten by 7.2 Lengths. Three horses stand out as a potential investment listed below.

Horse	Course	Value	Table Position	Beaten By
Samrouge	Laytown	6K	10th	8.5L
Maggie Thunder	Tipperary	6K	4th	2.1L
Below Deck	Curragh	8K	3rd	9.7L

Maggie Thunder coming from a track that is 4th in the table looks a good proposition Below Deck also looks interesting. With Samrouge coming from Laytown we know we are getting value for money there. the result is below.
1st: Samrouge 9/2
2nd: Below Deck 50/1
8th Maggie Thunder 25/1
There was only a Neck splitting the first two home, Below Deck was an excellent Value for Money Investment.

For All Weather racing taking horses that ran on an All-Weather course then returned on an All-Weather Course there is very little difference between the top of the table and the bottom. The fact that there is a difference though slight it is still worth noting if you are a Betting Shop punter the table is set out below.

Chelmsford City
Lingfield
Newcastle
Kempton Park
Southwell
Wolverhampton
Dundalk
Laytown

Again, Laytown though bottom of the table is the only track to show a level stake profit on all runners coming from Laytown to another track. This is because Laytown is vastly under estimated and the prices of runners from Laytown often represent good value for money.

All this being said. it is risky hobby just relying on courses previously raced on to make an investment. The Racing Post is a minefield of information if you have the time to digest it all. The ratings they give for each race also seem to be fairly good. However, you cannot compare with other data as easily as you can with software that is data orientated.

National Hunt Racing

NH Racing

NH Racing has always held a fascination for me, it is where I started my interest in Racing. As a betting medium it is the trickiest of the three disciplines to make any firm commitment on the outcome of any given race. What makes it tricky is that there is far more to go wrong. Your horse could fall, or get brought down, being a mainly winter sport the going is often heavy or at best Good to Soft, the weight the horses are carrying is greater than they carry on the flat, to emphasise the point a recent six race card at Market Rasen, three of the six races were won by horses that pulled up in their previous race. Any ratings or speed figures are unreliable for the race, you would need to go back to the horse's penultimate race to check for ability. One of the three winners Pulled Up in his last three races prior to his current race. How do you evaluate that form?

You may find that ratings for the reasons outlined above, also speed ratings are not so reliable. If I check a Handicap Hurdle race I would also check the other Hurdle races run on the same course on the same day, even if over a different distance, I would take the average time either above standard or below, divide it by the number of furlongs to try and get a comparison between the different distances. This helps with deciding if the rating is beneficial or not.

Everything written in this book about Flat Racing and All-Weather Racing applies to National Hunt too, including "Days of The Week" In handicap races horses that won their previous race and return on a Monday, win 23% of the time. However, horses that return on a Saturday, only win 14% of the time, which is what you might expect with the higher-class races being run on a Saturday. The difference in SP returns though is substantial. In non-handicaps horses that win their previous race and return on Monday win 33.63% of the time. When they return on a Saturday, they only win 25% of the time.

National Hunt Racing

You could produce many different systems to analyse why this happens, including finding losing systems.

For example, if you followed horses that win their previous race then start favourite for their next race. coupled with trainers that pull a second win off 40% or more of the time. that shows a profit at SP of £5K to a £10 stake over the last ten-year period. Obviously on the other side of the coin trainers whose horses start favourite after winning their previous but only manage to win less than 20% of the time show a huge loss. This gives you an opportunity to look for something else in the race that will be better value than the favourite. Of course, you will not always find a qualifying runner, and you should not just take a risk.

Sifting through data for National Hunt Racing, particularly trainer profiles could be rewarding.

Favourites in Handicaps is also worth considering. If you look at all Handicap races hurdles and chases over the last fifteen years you will see a pattern that could make you look beyond the favourite or take a good look at the favourite. I have printed a table on the following page that demonstrates this. The average win rate of the favourite in handicaps is 29.17%. You will see from the table if the favourite is also top weight, they win 31.88% of the time. The success rate drops off the further down the weight table they are. If they are fourteenth in the table, they only win 19.3% of the time. This gives us an advantage as we can see that once the favourite is below fourth in the weight table, they win less than the average amount of times. The further they are down the table the more it is worth looking for something that will be better value. We could break these figures down further to hurdles and chases, going etc. You could also do it on a course-by-course basis though the data would be lower to make a true comparison. The situation is the similar for flat racing and even more so for All-Weather racing.

National Hunt Racing

Position in Weight table	Bets	Wins	Percentage
1	7179	2289	31.88%
2	5456	1688	30.94%
3	4793	1398	29.17%
4	4169	1249	29.96%
5	3402	985	28.95%
6	2708	760	28.07%
7	2011	515	25.61%
8	1436	361	25.14%
9	972	254	26.13%
10	679	155	22.83%
11	425	101	23.76%
12	272	65	23.90%
13	157	36	22.93%
14	114	22	19.30%

Favourites that were fifth or lower in the weight table once went twenty-five races in row without a win, the highest wins in a row from favourites that were fifth or lower in the weights table is seven.

You can see from these percentages alone there are ways to turn the advantage in your favour. you should always be looking at systems like this to see if you can find value elsewhere. You do always need to make sure you can justifiably discount the favourite if following a system like this.

Summing Up

Summing Up

There is quite a bit of information in this book to digest. I have only scratched the surface with what could be achieved with software like Horseracebase or any of the other software packages with the ability to manipulate data.

As I have said previously working with too many systems is impossible. Following about 5 is probably the most reliable until you can understand how each one works to produce the most reliable results.

When I am not at the course, I like to look for losing systems more than winning ones, that gives me the opportunity to look for something that gives me better value.

For example, as I write today 18/10/2023 in my list of trainers that do not manage to get two winners in a row very often, there are 2 selections in the 3:10 Nottingham Amayretto and in the 2:52 Bath Connie Rose. Whose trainer has only managed to get 2 in row when they have started favourite on the 2nd occasion 9% of the time. In the Nottingham race I could not find another horse that I thought was worthwhile. In the Bath race I did find one that I thought could well be worth doing a bit more work on. I have printed the Ratings table of that race on the following page as it brings in other things we have run through earlier in the book.

Just as a reminder, Horseracebase show 20 columns of information in their ratings table, I am only printing 4 of them here as they are the most relevant for the things I look for.

It may be worth at this point looking at the table on the following page to see if you can spot what caught my eye in the first instance.

Summing Up

Wed 18th Oct 2023
2.52 Bath (14 runners)
Download The Vickers.Bet App Handicap
5½f (1260 yards)
Class 5, Soft, 3yo+, Win: £3873

Horse	Total	Odds	LR
Connies Rose	168.0	9/2	93.6
Apache Star (IRE)	162.2	9/2	73.2
Sarahs Verse	158.0	13/2	69
Symbol of Hope	148.0	12/1	61.1
Vinaka (IRE)	142.5	9/1	74.4
Concierge (IRE)	133.6	10/1	43.7
Hey Mr	126.9	14/1	59.6
Autum Angel (IRE)	124.6	11/1	49.4
Kitbag	123.4	8/1	60.3
Ultramarine (IRE)	119.6	15/2	46.2
Giddy Aunt	117.5	22/1	61.4
Fair And Square	114.3	66/1	38.8
Conquest Of Power	112.9	28/1	54.4
Kwiz (IRE)	74.7	200/1	37.4

Summing Up

As always, the table is listed by the Totals column, when we look at the runners ratings last time out two horses stood out to me. Working our way up from the bottom which I have mentioned before Giddy Aunt's rating of 61.4 stands out as being out of line with the Totals column. She has a better rating than 6 horses above her. The other who looked slightly interesting is Vinaka.

The Favourite Connies Rose is ahead on her last race with a rating of 93.6 but I now know that her trainer rarely strings 2 wins together particularly when they start favourite in their current race.

I watched the previous races of the majority of the runners and I was well impressed with the way Giddy Aunt stuck to the task to get beaten by two short heads. I was not impressed by the heavy wacks she got in the straight and I think pity stopped me supporting her today. She ran out a comfortable winner of today's race at 22/1 without getting the aforementioned encouragement from the saddle. Vinaka was fourth at 9/1.

The other pointer for Giddy Aunt was that her trainer has his best winning percentage as many trainers do when the horse returns to the course within 7 days. She was also wearing cheek pieces for the first time which also can bring out some improvement in a horse.

In the chapter on Favourites, I also mentioned keeping a list of trainers whose horses win but do not follow up no matter where they are in the market. There was a runner that came up today obviously the two I have just mentioned came up too. This is no matter where they are in the market this horse also started favourite. She did not come up in the Favourite system because the trainer does not have enough favourites to come into that system, she gets covered in this one, this again is a system looking for losers. The table is printed on the following page.

Summing Up

Wed 18th Oct 2023
5.10 Bath (6 runners)
BLTH Fillies Handicap
1m (1760 yards)
Class 5, Heavy, 3yo+, Win: £3873

Horse	Total	Odds	LR
Albus Anne	305.2	8/11	86.8
Big Beat Hug	268.1	85/40	64.9
Tilt AT Windmills (IRE)	236.5	16/1	74.0
Motasaleeta	230.9	28/1	46.0
Medina Gold (FR)	211.4	13/2	41.3
Love Whisper (IRE)	164.8	100/1	18.1

Just for completeness there were three non-runners in this race with two of them being taken out just one hour before the race.
The table is from my 100% ratings. The favourite Albus Anne is trained by a trainer who is in my list of trainers that rarely puts two wins together. In fact, this trainer to date has never achieved it. Tilt At Windmills has the third best rating also has a good rating last time out. She also has a slightly better Speed Rating than Albus Anne. She carries 6lb less than last time therefore her speed rating could improve. Albus Anne carries 3lb more than her last race she also won her last race on a Monday. The scene was set for Tilt At Windmills to run a big race, and so she did, winning at 16/1.

That is a 16/1 and a 22/1 winner on the same day using systems looking for losers.

Summing Up

The win rate for trainers winning twice on the bounce in Ireland is slightly less at 15.22%, but the same rules apply. Keep records for trainers above say 20% and trainers below 12%, beware of the top trainers though as their horses are at restricted prices.

Of course, you do not have to just look for trainers to find losing systems you could look at Stallions whose prodigy win rate tails off over or under certain distances. Or stallions whose prodigy do not perform well on certain types of going or even on left or right-handed tracks. The list is endless as to what you could do.

If we take a stallion that has a lot of prodigies like Dubawi we can instantly see his highest percentage of winners come from 7 furlongs to 1 mile and 3 furlongs. Anything outside those distances his win rate drops off remarkably. over 1 mile his prodigies wins about 23% of the time, over 5 Furlongs they only win 11% of the time.

Today Dubawi had one of his prodigies running at Bath trained by John Gosden she was racing over 1Mile 6 Furlongs. Not a good distance for a Dubawi horse, she started the 9/4 favourite and finished third beaten by the second favourite. A Galileo (IRE) who's prodigy perform right up to 1 mile 6 Furlongs before they tail off.

An interesting fact when looking at Stallions is that when a Frankel prodigy runs on going anything softer than Good to Soft there win rate drops off a cliff. Also, his prodigies win rate on the All Weather is only about 17% compared to 23% on Good to Firm going. I say only 17%, that is better than most Stallions.

I could go on and on about stallions and their strengths and weaknesses you can find that information for yourselves. It is massively untouched area for investing on horses. I could draft books full of information and samples of races for all sorts of data. You do not need me to do that, you can do it for yourselves using programmes like Horseracebase.

Summing Up

To sum up there is no easy way to success. Also, there is not just one way to be successful. You need to put in the work being lazy and not covering all bases is not the answer. A rule of thumb is, if you only spend 10 minutes on the runners of a particular race then you are not checking the race out thoroughly, I expect to spend a hour or more to check all the angles, review all the contestants previous races etc. I may leave the race and return to it again if needs be. The more you put into it the luckier you will be there is plenty to learn. I could write a book on every chapter in this book. I have only scratched the surface here to show what can be achieved. Go racing as often as possible and if you see someone standing alone by the pre parade ring whilst the previous race is being run, it will probably be me. So come up and say hello and we can chew the cud.

All the best for now.

Isaac Robathan.

Some old Horse and Trainer notes

I have added some trainer notes and horse notes that I made some time ago. They would have all changed many times since but it shows you what sort of notes you can keep.

Old Horse Notes

Swiss Chill	040618 Windsor can do better and will show improvement.
Take Fright	060618 Kempton pre-empted the stalls opening and got behind very good late headway
Team Decision (IRE)	240518 Chelmsford improved here first three clear
Terrier Spirit (IRE)	020618 Doncaster Debut run slow away pulled his way to the front and bolted in.
That Is The Spirit	100617 Led all the way and stuck to the inside rail where the ground was not so good all others tracked over to better ground. 6f would suit better.
The Last Party	280518 Chelmsford broke well from stall 1 had the run of the race wandered at the finish and may not be so lucky next time Oppose if possible

Just a few Old Trainer Notes

Cantillon, D E	Does not have many horses but clearly knows his stuff 20% over all 50% place horses rarely run a bad a race and can definitely bounce back after a bad race
Carr, Mrs R A	Best when horses have had a run March 2018 recently turning winners out even after a long break, 7 days or less 14% Win 40% place
Carroll, A W	Horse generally improve after first run from a break, Watch for horses dropping from a 3K to a 2K race
Channon, M R	Uses apprentices to good effect, not good after a Break. But watch for horses in their 3rd and 4th races after a break or from first time out

Trainers

Watson,Archie (Trainer Notes) 18% winners prolific place
getter, Can improve horses taken over from other trainers. All
horses on their 2nd or 3rd run need to be looked at very closely.
Even if moved up in class particularly top class on 3rd run from
break.

Owens, Patrick (Trainer Notes) Decent trainer, when he gets
a win with a 2yo or 3yo tends to jump them too high and just
fails, needs more checking

Holland, Darryll (Trainer Notes) Drop in class and/or prize
money is very significant, a drop-in OR is worth noting, as the OR
gets higher they lose their form. when finishing out of 1st three but
close up they are worth a second look

Scott, George (Trainer Notes) 16% winners overall, one to
be watched and checked. September 22 still okish, 1st run 3%, if
he runs a 2yo in a higher class race first time out, he thinks
something of it, watch when dropped in class. Horses maintain
their form if kept to same class

Fahey, R A (Trainer Notes) very reliable, Richards when
slowly away or in rear 1st time out will always improve next time.
non handicappers could do it 2nd time out if accompanied by a
drop a class, June 23 2yo, are winning first time out currently.

Easterby, T D (Trainer Notes) Horses can be well btn in 3 mdns,
then dropped in class for 1st hcp and win at a decent price, you
really have to take note of Tims horses being dropped in class and
prize money, even if finishing last in a bigger race, often win or run
well at big prices.

Murphy, Amy (Trainer Notes) Watch for a change of head gear
she knows her stuff with headgear

Cox, C G	Can win after a break but nearly always improve for a run. Exceptional when 7 runners or less. Particularly when Adam Kirby is up.
Craggs, R	watch for horses 2nd or third run from break can often come in at big prices particularly if drop in class and/or claimer ridden.
Crisford, Simon	very good trainer, horses are definitely worth a look at, 15% first time out winners, very good win and place ratio. Maidens dropped in class of course 2nd or third run often do the business, can certainly Ready a horse, Watch for 1st time in Hcps
Crowley, Miss Jo	150413 Low % Trainer 10% horses not firing 15/4 1rnr 7/1 tailed off
Cumani, L M	No problem with horses after a breakup to 20% win
Curran, S	profit from flat horses, can produce a horse after a break and run up a sequence
Curtis, R	140413 Low % trainer horses not yet performing
Dartnall, V R A	110413 Place average poor, but horses running up to and better than expected at the mo. Does not have many short priced favs but when he does they do NOT do well recently
Davis, D J S Ffrench	Fancied horses are worth looking at, they rarely disappoint, mdns finishing 2nd or very close 1st time out often win at short prices next time. Can move horses up in class without a problem. Excellent trainer.

Some old horse notes

Shine So Bright	100618 Nottingham Looked to win a decent race quite easily here.
Silk Mill Blue	220618 Wetherby Ran very wide from a bad draw, was putting in some decent work at the end, a smaller field and better draw he will do well.
Sirius Slew	180618 Carlisle Ran green will improve
Snowdon	080518 Thirsk looked much better than her final placing suggests, has run again at Doncaster 190518 still better than this result. 070618 Bolted in at Yarmouth and is much better than his handicap mark.
Storm Melody	020618 Chepstow did not look to try a yard until it was well to late and is definitely better than this. on 2nd look it looks to have been a pretty poor race
Straight Ash (IRE)	Ran on really well at the death at Leicester 29/05/18 maybe better on turf than AW
Stylistique	120919 Doncaster, looked one of the best in the paddock and ran accordingly
Summerghand (IRE)	280718 York raced at the back and kept coming through the field doing the best at the end from the unfavoured stand side
Sun Maiden	170518 Salisbury The way the runner ran next time out Sun Maiden must be very good
Swift Wing	050919 Haydock: seem to remember there was still something to be worked on so should improve.